D1093639

**This Book is a Gift to the
Jackson County Library System
From
Southern Oregon
Antiques & Collectibles Club**

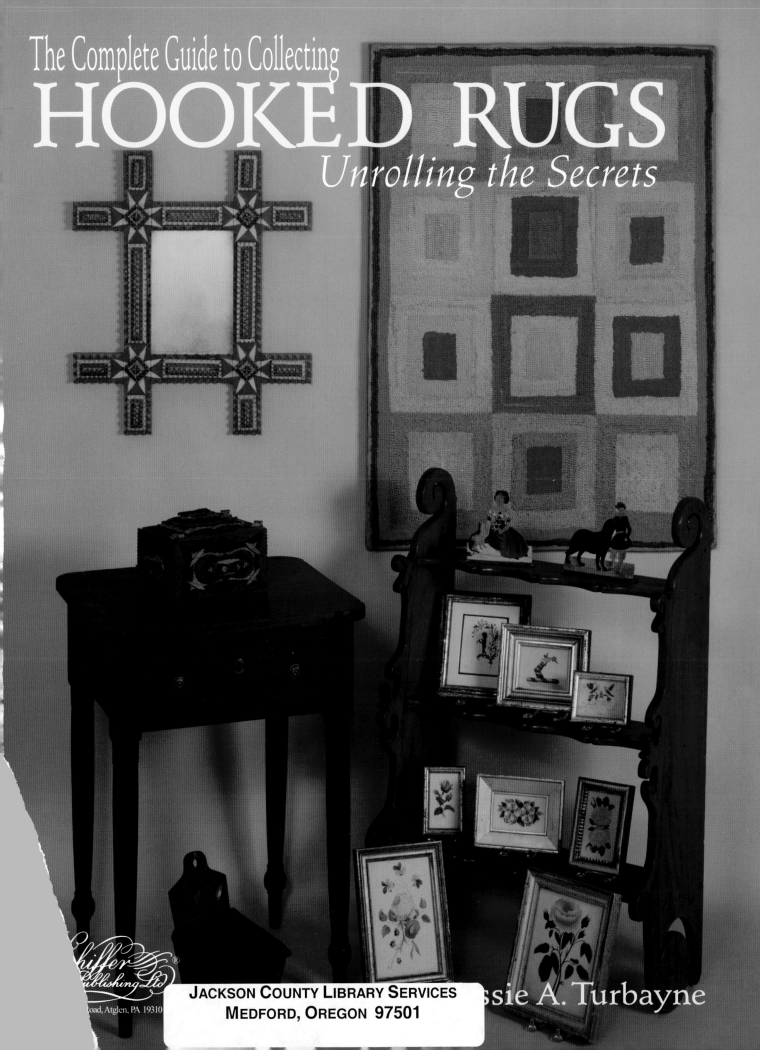

The Complete Guide to Collecting

HOOKED RUGS
Unrolling the Secrets

Jessie A. Turbayne

Schiffer
Publishing Ltd®

Road, Atglen, PA 19310

Library of Congress Cataloging-in-Publication Data

Turbayne, Jessie A.
The complete guide to collecting hooked rugs : unrolling the secrets / by Jessie A. Turbayne.
p. cm.
ISBN 0-7643-1954-X (Hardcover)
1. Rugs, Hooked--Collectors and collecting. 2. Rugs, Hooked--North America. I. Title.
NK2795.T87 2004
746.7'4'075--dc22
2003016031

Designed by Bonnie M. Hensley
Cover design by Bruce Waters
Type set in Hallmarke Lt/Zurich LtCn BT

ISBN: 0-7643-1954-X
Printed in China
1 2 3 4

Published by Schiffer Publishing Ltd.
4880 Lower Valley Road
Atglen, PA 19310
Phone: (610) 593-1777; Fax: (610) 593-2002
E-mail: Info@schifferbooks.com
Please visit our web site catalog at **www.schifferbooks.com**
We are always looking for people to write books on new and related subjects. If you have an idea for a book please contact us at the above address.

This book may be purchased from the publisher.
Include $3.95 for shipping. Please try your bookstore first. You may write for a free catalog.

In Europe, Schiffer books are distributed by
Bushwood Books
6 Marksbury Ave.
Kew Gardens
Surrey TW9 4JF England
Phone: 44 (0) 20 8392-8585; Fax: 44 (0) 20 8392-9876
E-mail: Bushwd@aol.com
Free postage in the U.K., Europe; air mail at cost.

Dedication

To Jamie who taught me at an early age to look beyond life's holes and frayed edges and see beauty.

To Michael whose love and strength patches up life's holes and soothes my frayed edges.

There's no place like home. Grenfell Labrador Industries. Early 20th century. 6" diameter.

Acknowledgments

I wish to extend my sincere gratitude to those who contributed to the making of this book. A very special word of thanks to my editors, Nancy Schiffer and Douglas Congdon-Martin, Peter Schiffer, and Schiffer Publishing Ltd. I am also grateful to electrical engineer, fellow rug hooker, and friend Judy Yasi who not only saved my sanity, but rescued my computer from an isolated but deadly case of the sledge hammer virus. Kind acknowledgments to Jeanne Benjamin / New Earth Designs; Jane C. Blanchard, Jeremiah Dalton House Antiques, Wiscasset, Maine; Jeff R. Bridgman Antiques, Mansfield, Pennsylvania; Dorothy Brown; Mary Sheppard Burton; Linda Rae Coughlin; Jeanie Crockett; Liz Alpert Fay; Ethan Firestone: Cindi Gay; Russ and Karen Goldberger, RJG Antiques, Rye, New Hampshire; Jan Hale, Corn Crib Antiques, Henniker, New Hampshire; Rae Reynolds Harrell; Hawks Nest Antiques, Hinesburg, Vermont; Cathy Henning; Highfields Antiques, St. Albans, Maine; Gail H. Horton; Trish Johnson; Susan and Samuel Keith; Stephanie Ashworth Krauss; H. B. Leddy; Peter Lee; Rosalie Lent; Roslyn Logsdon; Margaret Arraj MacDonald; McAdoo Rugs, North Bennington, Vermont; Marjorie Mello; Sybil Mercer, Pat Merikallio; Michele Micarelli; June Mikoryak; Jo-Ann Millen; R. Jesse Morley; Scott Morrison, SDS Computers, Walpole, Massachusetts; Claire Morton; The Moshimer Family and W. Cushing and Company, Kennebunkport, Maine; Christopher Moutenot; Northeast Auctions, Portsmouth, New Hampshire; Rita O'Neill; The Ontario Hooking Craft Guild; Susan Page, Lincoln, Massachusetts; Christine Parker; Deanie Pass; Mary Jane Patchell; Mark Perry and Dee DiNallo; Rob Petta; Diane Phillips; Denise Reithofer; Reynolds Photography; June Robbs; Emily K. Robertson; Francis Sanagan; Michael Santos; Sauder Village, Archbold, Ohio; Stephen and Eleanor Score; Iris Simpson; Susan Smidt; Annie A. Spring; Brad Stanton; Sidney and Elizabeth Stewart; Denny L Tracey; Anthony and Florence Travis; C. Allan Turbayne; James A Turbayne; Justina Rae Two Eagle; Wendy Ullmann; Leah Christine Runci-Valerie; The Wenham Museum, Wenham, Massachusetts; Margaret Hunt Wilson and Rose Wirtz.

Contents

Introduction

The act of collecting can be very personal; a reflection of one's self. It awakens our senses yet soothes an innate yearning to gather together that which we desire. It is a learning process for all, a full time occupation for many, and a pleasurable hobby for millions.

The key to building a great collection is to be knowledgeable about what you collect. An educated buyer is a smart buyer. This book will provide you with the tools needed to make wise choices when it comes to purchasing hooked rugs. As your collection grows you will be rewarded aesthetically, spiritually, and if you wish to sell, monetarily.

For over 30 years I've enjoyed a full time career of restoring, buying, selling, and collecting hooked rugs. The following pages clearly illustrate why I plan on continuing to collect for the next 30 years.

Red curlicue scrolls and a grand floral wreath overpower the central image of an untitled book; miniature in scale and perhaps an afterthought. 1900-1920. 32" x 52".

Note: Hooked rug measurements have been rounded to the nearest half of an inch. Height precedes width. Ages assigned to the rugs have been supplied by their owners or are to the best of my knowledge. All antique and collectible rugs are hooked on burlap unless otherwise noted. All contemporary rugs are hooked on burlap, rug hooking linen, monk's cloth or other cotton foundations. In some cases of special interest, the hooking materials have been listed. All hooked rugs are made in the United States unless otherwise noted. Those hooked rugs, mats, and related items to which no acknowledgment has been ascribed belong to the author.

Tumbling blocks create an optical illusion. 1910-1920. 33.5" x 54". *Courtesy of Mark Perry and Dee DiNallo.*

A decorative motif centuries old, the pattern of intertwining rope is timeless. "Antique Twist." June Robbs. 1997. 39" x 57". *Courtesy of June Robbs.*

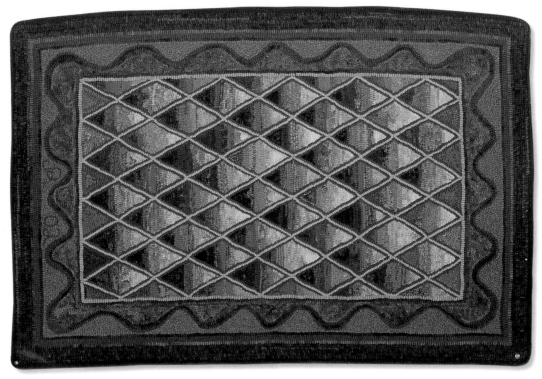

Jewel-like diamonds form the centerpiece of "Great Masters Geometric," a design adapted from an antique rug. June Robbs. 2002. 28" x 41". *Courtesy of June Robbs*.

Close-up of "Great Masters Geometric." *Courtesy of June Robbs*.

Chapter One

Why Collect Hooked Rugs?

That irregular and intimate quality of things made entirely by the human hand.
—Willa Cather

Why collect hooked rugs? As functioning art they are equally at home hung on walls as placed on floors. Pleasing to the eye and gentle on the foot, there are few that can resist the charm of a hand-hooked rug or can ignore the fact that prices of hooked rugs have steadily risen over the past thirty years.

As functioning art hooked rugs are equally at home hung on the wall as placed on the floor. The gallery of RJG Antiques. *Courtesy of Russ and Karen Goldberger/ RJG Antiques, Rye, New Hampshire.*

Art under foot. "Jerico." Designed by Marion Ham and hooked by June Robbs. 1999. 6.5' x 8'. *Courtesy of June Robbs.*

"If It's Not One Thing It's Your Mother." A work in progress by hooked rug designer and teacher, Jeanne Benjamin. *Courtesy of Jeanne Benjamin / New Earth Designs.*

Hooked rugs enhance any décor by adding color, texture, and warmth.

This small mat, hooked by the author, was inspired by early 20th century American Indian trade blankets and made to honor a friendship with a special little girl, Justina Rae Two Eagle. 2001. 23.5" x 24.5".

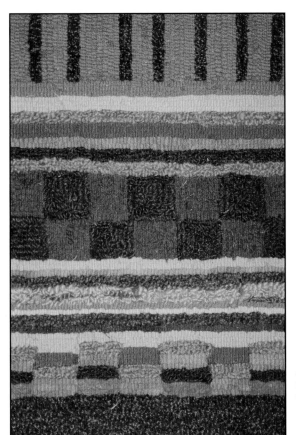

Tools of the trade; a variety of fabrics, hook, scissors, and cut up strips.

A close-up of the aforementioned hooked mat reveals the variety of materials used including as is woolen fabrics and homespun woolen yarns; natural black and dyed with walnut hulls.

Chapter Two

What Type of Hooked Rugs to Collect

So now that you're hooked, do you purchase all that you see or select rugs of a certain age or theme? Buying just for the sake of buying is unwise and costly. Focusing on a particular type or age of hooked rug is a good way to start a collection.

Hooked rugs with lush roses and ornate scrolls are right at home in Victorian houses. Geometric and abstract patterns complement simple country furniture as well as sleek modern pieces. Can't afford Oriental rugs? Ingenious rug hookers of the past and present mimic hand knotted carpets with remarkable success. For those who have a newfound interest in Arctic exploration, Grenfell mats hooked in Newfoundland and Labrador will satisfy your craving for polar bears, dog teams, and icebergs. Women and men started making hooked rugs in the 1850s and they haven't stopped hooking yet. Dogs, cats, and horses, houses, landscapes, seascapes, and printed verse, primitive, realistic, and abstract; the list of hooked subject matter goes on and on. Antique, collectible or contemporary; the choice is yours. Collect what you like but be knowledgeable about what you collect.

Resplendent scrolls elegantly frame a garden fresh bouquet. "Challenge." A Pearl McGown pattern hooked by June Mikoryak. 1982. 29" x 49". *Courtesy of June Mikoryak.*

Regardless of what age or type you choose, make sure your rugs have character. A rug with character will capture your attention, awaken the senses, and challenge your intellect through use of design, color, and skill. Hooked rugs are like paintings. There are good ones and there are bad ones.

Roses blend harmoniously with buds and blooms of unknown floral species. Hooked entirely of woolen yarns and framed with a braided border. 1880-1900. 32" x 50". *Courtesy of Sidney and Elizabeth Stewart.*

"Wild Flowers of Portugal" was inspired by a photograph taken when Canadian rug hooker Sybil Mercer visited this scenic European country. To replicate the sheen from the sun some of the blossoms were hooked using silk embroidery floss. Sybil Mercer. 1999. 12" x 22". *Courtesy of Sybil Mercer.*

Triangles, fancy and few, mingle with their plain companions. Concentric rectangles and a braided border frame the interior design. 1890-1910. 33" x 62".

Although carefree in appearance the execution of a well done abstract design requires careful planning. "Motif # 47". From the Anne Tuckaway-Doodlin Motif Collection. Designed and hooked by Annie A. Spring. 1997. 14" x 11". *Courtesy of Annie A. Spring.*

"Temple Bells," an Oriental inspired design by Joan Moshimer and hooked by Dorothy Brown. 2002. 27" x 48.5". *Courtesy of Dorothy Brown.*

Detail of "Temple Bells." Rug maker Dorothy Brown hand-dyed all the woolen fabrics she hooked. *Courtesy of Dorothy Brown.*

Hooked and sold by the Grenfell Labrador Industries during the early 20th century, this fine example of a Grenfell mat depicting a polar bear at water's edge would be a welcomed addition to any collection. 40.5" x 26". *Private Collection.*

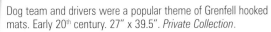

Dog team and drivers were a popular theme of Grenfell hooked mats. Early 20th century. 27" x 39.5". *Private Collection.*

Folk art at its best. Amid houses and lollipop trees, twin riders straddle oversized cats. Jute twine was vertically hooked to create the ochre background. 1900-1920. 18" x 35".

This "Fat Cat" looks like he swallowed more than just the canary. Patsy Becker design. Hooked by Canada's own Cathy Henning. 2000. 30" x 20". *Courtesy of Cathy Henning.*

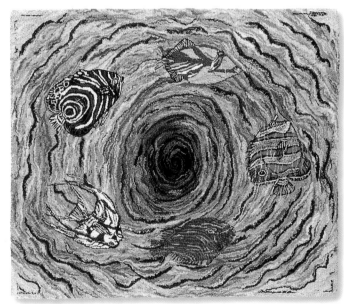

Fish in a frenzy try to swim against a "Whirl Poole." Susan Smidt. 1995. 32.5" x 38". *Courtesy of Susan Smidt.*

Serenity can be found in a cabin amongst the pines. Or is that a palm tree? 1920-1940. Diameter 15".

"Planes In Space" is the combined effort of artist Jamie O'Neill and his rug hooking grandmother Rita O'Neill. 2002. 31.5" x 41". *Courtesy of Rita O'Neill.*

Chapter Three

Age Options

When it comes to dating hooked rugs there are three age categories: antique, collectible, and antique. Each group has distinctive attributes.

ANTIQUE HOOKED RUGS: 100 YEARS PLUS

Design elements, colors, fabrics used, and the signs of wear and tear validate the vintage of this yarn hooked rug dated 1881. 29" x 52".

Centennial hooked rugs celebrated 100 years of our country's independence. 1870-1890. Dimensions unavailable. *Courtesy of Mark Perry and Dee DiNallo.*

To be deemed in antique, in the United States, a hooked rug must be at least 100 years old. Accurate dating can be difficult. Few were signed and dated or given a maker's label. It is highly unusual to locate antique hooked rugs with documented provenance. After studying the design, style of hooking, and, most importantly, the fabrics and foundation used and signs of wear, an educated opinion is formed to determine the rug's approximate age. Often the term circa is used when exact dating is impossible.

Antique hooked rugs evoke images of simpler times; of family, home, and a slower pace of living. Used to warm and decorate drafty floors, rugs, hooked from discarded clothing of family and friends, were often regarded as objects of great sentimental value. Though crafted by both sexes, many were the means of creative expression for women during times when female voices and opinions were not always heard. Designed by the maker or worked from preprinted patterns, hooked rugs reflected the styles and trends of a past era. They serve as an interesting and informative textile time line. Choice antique hooked rugs in good condition command high prices.

An ornate center field true to Victorian style gives way to a border of simpler design. In need of minor repair but charming nonetheless. Dated 1885 and of the period. 29" x 49". *Courtesy of Sidney and Elizabeth Stewart.*

Flowers That Never Wilt

Antique dealers and collectors, Mark Perry and Dee DiNallo of Massachusetts' own Nantucket Island give us a glimpse into their hooked folk art garden. Each year through selective buying and selling the collection grows.

Bursting from an earthy patch, an array of eclectic flowers foretell the promise of spring. 1850-1860. 39" x 70". *Courtesy of Mark Perry and Dee DiNallo.*

A centrally located heart, complete with initials, signifies the union of two homes and honors a beloved bride and groom. Trees of life and flowers flank the centerpiece. Wool and cotton fabrics on linen. 1840-1850. 33.5" x 75". *Courtesy of Mark Perry and Dee DiNallo.*

Depicted in grand style, a single stalk with multiple blooms and oversized leaves emerges from a simple vessel. Abstract forms, of perhaps a floral nature, compete for attention. 1890-1910. Dimensions unavailable. *Courtesy of Mark Perry and Dee DiNallo.*

Roses in triplicate form a center medallion. Sprays of buds and leaves project from each side in a mirror-like fashion. Elongated S-shaped scrolls frame the floral design. 1850-1870. 29" x 50". *Courtesy of Mark Perry and Dee DiNallo.*

COLLECTIBLE HOOKED RUGS

The largest number of hand-hooked rugs sold today fall into what is called the collectible category. The term collectible is often used when referring to rugs that can range anywhere from being 25 to 75 years old, though that span of time is not exact. Not old enough to be classified as antique or young enough to be considered contemporary, this diverse group of hooked rugs attracts a broad audience. Prices for collectible hooked rugs cover a wide range, but are generally lower then their antique counterparts.

A limited palette was used to fashion 60 blocks, no two alike. 1950-1970. 27" x 41".

Unsophisticated yet charming, this simple hooked rug was a flea market find and reasonable priced at $85. 1940-1960. 24" x 36".

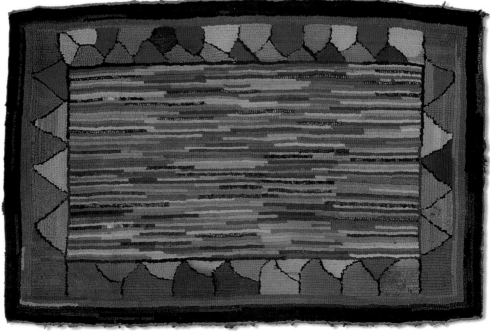

Diamond pinwheels by the pair line up to pave the way. A closer look reveals that each motif is unique. Among the many designs and symbols are initials, the date 1938, images of a cat and a man, and the logo for Chevrolet. 1930-1950. 10' x 28".

The maker of this rug not only combined the colors and designs of the southwest but hooked the background in a horizontal manner to mimic weaving. Due to the edge damage which can easily be remedied the rug was purchased for $50. A preprinted pattern. Of Canadian Maritime origins. 1950-1970. 19" x 31".

Hand-hooked rugs of impressive dimension are few and far between. Many yards of woolen fabric were hand cut into ¼" strips then hooked into a runner that could be used to carpet either a hall or stairway. 1930-1950. 22" x 17' 4".

Abstract art as interpreted by an unconventional rug hooker. 1930-1950. 26" x 36".

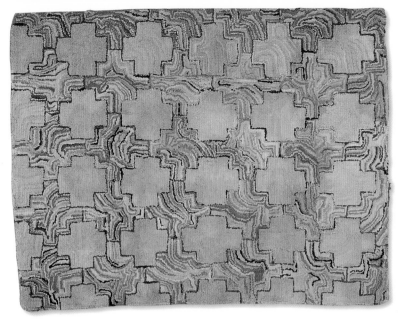

Rows of pale aqua crosses line up in formation on a striated field. Due to its irregular design pattern it appears that the rug was once larger and has been cut down. Closer examination of the front and back reveals that the rug maker simply hooked the design to fit the size of the burlap foundation and if part of the pattern was cut off so be it. 1920-1930. 38" x 48".

Not only were small mats quick and easy to hook but when finished added decorative touches of color to tabletops and bureaus. 1930-1950. 4" x 4".

Concentric rectangles frame this diminutive study of color and abstract design. 1920-1930. 13" x 15".

Simple yet striking. Narrow hooked runners complement floors, walls, and tables. 1910-1930. 18" x 54". *Private collection*.

Garrett's Blue Nose Rugs of Nova Scotia offered many preprinted patterns honoring fraternal organizations. The three-link chain is a symbol used by the Independent Order of Odd Fellows. Of Canadian Maritime origins. 1930-1950. 30" x 52".

Ornate scroll work dominates a striated neutral field. A preprinted pattern. 1940-1950. 30" x 51".

More scrolls; these incorporating a leaf motif. Hooked entirely of woolen yarns. A preprinted pattern. Of Canadian Maritime origins. 1940-1960. 30" x 50".

Blossoms of red and yellow rest upon a background of navy and purple. 1940-1950. 21" x 36".

Rug hookers create with ease what botanists have tried to grow; a purple rose. A preprinted pattern. 1940-1950. 24" x 36".

Delicate peach colored rose and bud were hooked to decorate a special chair. A preprinted pattern. 1940-1960. 14" x 12".

An assortment of blooms, leaves, and bare twigs frame oversized bright red poppies. A preprinted pattern. 1960-1970. 25" x 45".

Stylized flowers bring color and cheer to a striped field. A preprinted pattern. 1950-1970. 22" x 36".

An unusual combination of colors was used to hook daisy-like flowers and buds. Hooked from a preprinted pattern using wool and cotton jersey fabrics. 1950-1960. 18" x 28".

A home any cartoon character would be proud to call their own. Fashioned from yarn using a shuttle type hook. A preprinted pattern. 1940-1960. 24" x 36".

Space a problem? Collect miniature mats such as this tiny hooked image of a house. Originally intended for use under a beverage. Of Canadian origins. 1930-1950. 3" x 3".

The family homestead in need of a few repairs. A preprinted Garrett's Blue Nose rug pattern with an added duck. Of Canadian Maritime origins. 1930-1950. 28" x 57".

A Garrett's Blue Nose rug pattern of a stately stag was transformed into a whimsical portrait of Rudolf, the red nosed reindeer. Of mixed materials on burlap with twine hooked antlers. Of Canadian Maritime origins. 1940-1950. 25" x 40".

Scottie dogs, made popular by President Franklin D. Roosevelt's own Fala, appeared on many hooked rugs. Vines, buds, and four flowers with raised and sculpture centers frame this mustard colored pet. A preprinted pattern. 1940-1950. 24" x 38".

Year's end means slim picking for two hungry squirrels. 1910-1930. 31" x 50". *Private Collection*. 8".

A crazy quilt collage of favorite things was hooked by Ethel Fitzgerald, aunt of the late actor, Rock Hudson. A preprinted pattern. 1950-1960. 37" x 48".

Where the spirit does not work with the hand, there is no art.
—Leonardo Da Vinci

Today's rug hooking artists still create with a hook and strips of fabric or yarn as earlier rug makers did, but for many the intended goal has changed. In addition to those who hook rugs for floor use, there is a new generation of hooking artists whose work will never witness the underside of a shoe. No longer confined to using recycled fabrics (though many still do with superb results) contemporary hooking artists are able to choose from an ever-growing palette of fabrics and yarns of seemingly endless colors and textures. Their work catches your attention, challenges your mind, and stimulates the senses much like a fine painting or sculpture does. Prices reflect the artist's talent and the public's demand.

"The Offering" by Canadian artist Denise Reithofer is an example of contemporary hooked art at its best. 2000. 45" x 41". *Courtesy of Denise Reithofer.*

A closer look of "The Offering." *Courtesy of Denise Reithofer*.

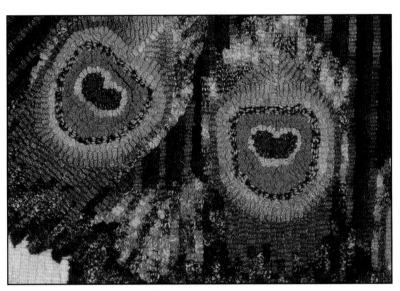

Detail of "The Offering." *Courtesy of Denise Reithofer*.

Detail of "The Offering." *Courtesy of Denise Reithofer*

Contemporary hooking artists are able to choose from a rainbow palette of hand-dyed woolen fabrics. *Courtesy of Jeanne Benjamin / New Earth Designs*.

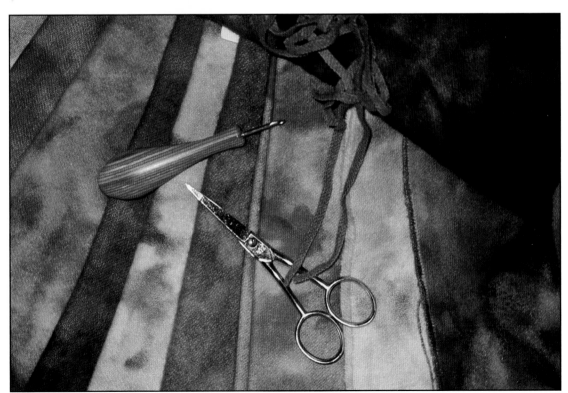

Deanie Pass, Minneapolis, Minnesota

Traditional narrative hooked rugs have always had a duality between function and non-function. An early rug, hooked by a whaler and illustrating the harpooning of an unfortunate whale, not only warmed a special someone's hearth, but also narrated the whaler's drama at sea. I have continued in this narrative folk art vein, illustrating my daily dramas. Within my rugs I'm the center of my world. My rugs play off references to art and art history. Often, I use humor to emphasize a relationship between word and image.

Today the majority of rug hookers unfortunately use patterns. They achieve their originality in their dyeing techniques. I prefer to use commercially dyed wool from second hand clothing. Because of my aversion to dyeing, I reinvented pointillism. When I began hooking the red tabletop in "Rugful of Good Fortune," I ran out of red wool. Instead of dyeing more, I dug through my laundry basket of

Pictured at work in her studio is hooking artist Deanie Pass and feline companion Moses. *Courtesy of Deanie Pass.*

strips pulled from previous work. The rug evolved one bit of color at a time. Since that rug I've continued using left over scraps to create impressionistic images. I prefer strong, often dramatic colors reminiscent of the Fauvists rather than the softer palette of the Impressionists.

Conventionally, narrative rugs have a center and border. Redefining this structure, I frequently surround the rug with words. In other rugs, the center is a stage or a circus, and the borders are replaced by curtains or tent flaps. Lately, I've incorporated braiding, another time-honored rug technique. The colorful braiding magnifies the center's hooked pointillism.

Hand-hooking is a slow process. The image is formed by thousands of loops. The repetitive process becomes a relaxed, meditative experience. By concentrating on each problem and solving them one by one, my rugs evolve slowly. I hook one rug at a time, completing one every two months. Obsessiveness is an obvious part of the process.

I create these rugs to be stepped on, walked on, and, more than likely, laid on by a pet or two. With reasonable care they can withstand decades. Just like the whaler's hooked rug, I hope my rugs tell their tales into the next century.

A sculptress turned rug hooking artist, the acclaimed works of Deanie Pass have been exhibited in museums, galleries, and one woman shows throughout the United States. And can be found in museum and private collections. Her work is represented by several galleries and is also available directly from the artist.

Featured here in chronological order is a selected portfolio of Deanie's work. The theme of many is centered on the humorous interpretation of a word or familiar saying. Others were inspired from a more serious side of life. In some cases it has been noted that the hooked piece was created with torn strips of woolen fabric. This technique, popular 100 years ago, is rarely used today. Most contemporary rug hookers rely on a hand-cranked or electric cutter to slice the strips of fabric they will hook.

The two worlds of husband Frank are portrayed in "Day And Night You Are the One." Deanie Pass. 1992. 38" x 52". *Courtesy of Deanie Pass.*

"Don't Tread on Me" recalls a saying of historical significance. Deanie Pass. 1993. 36" x 42". Gift to her son Zack Pass. *Courtesy of Deanie Pass.*

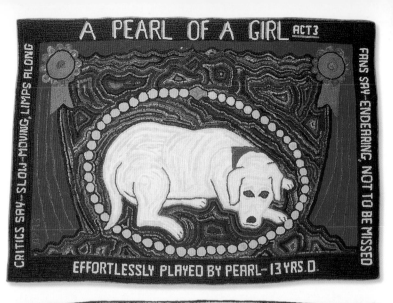

TOP TO BOTTOM:
"A Pearl Of A Girl," the star of the show, takes a 3rd act bow. Deanie Pass. 1993. 38.5" x 45". *Courtesy of Deanie Pass.*

One in a series of saying rugs. "Prayer Rug." 1994. 28" x 42". *Courtesy of Deanie Pass.*

Always check the weather report before taking the plunge. "It Was So Cold I Almost Got Married." Deanie Pass. 1994. 30" x 40". Gift to David Pass. *Courtesy of Deanie Pass.*

A bowl of fruit takes center stage in this hooked "Happy Mother's Day" greeting. Deanie Pass. 1995. 34" x 50". Gift to Anita Gerenraich. *Courtesy of Deanie Pass.*

Whether covering a floor or covering a head, "A Rug Is A Rug." Deanie Pass. 1995. 41" x 30". Gift to Frank Pass. *Courtesy of Deanie Pass.*

Jane bares it all over a spot of tea. "Jane's Bare Rug." 1996. 33" x 55". Commissioned by Jane Bassuk. *Courtesy of Deanie Pass.*

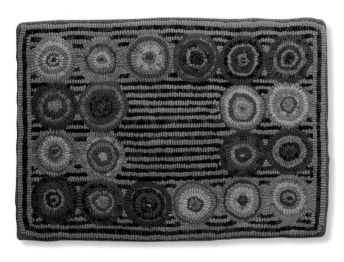

Having just been diagnosed with breast cancer, "Tilt-A-Whirl," the artist's only abstract, was hooked during a time of uncertainty. Deanie Pass. 1997. 12" x 18". Collection of Anita Kunin. *Courtesy of Deanie Pass.*

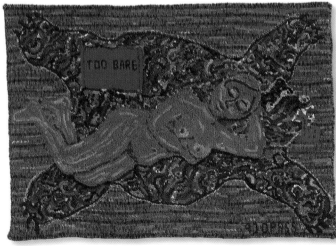

Bare against bear. "Too Bare." Torn wool on linen. Deanie Pass. 1997. 40" x 60". Commissioned by Heather Wallace. *Courtesy of Deanie Pass.*

A quick clean up guarantees time for soap operas. "Daytime Drama –Sweeping It Under The Rug." Torn wool on linen. Deanie Pass. 1997. Collection of Connee Mayeron Cowels. *Courtesy Deanie Pass*.

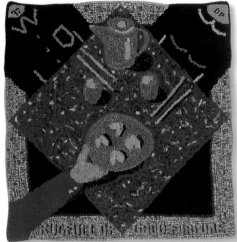

An overhead view of tea for two brings wishes of good fortune. "Rugful of Good Fortune" was hooked after the artist's successful treatment for breast cancer. 1997. 38" x 38". *Courtesy of Deanie Pass*.

"As Snug As A Bug In A Rug." A good book and the warmth of a roaring fire are shared on a snowy winter's night. Torn wool strips on linen. Deanie Pass. 1998. 39.5" x 43". *Courtesy of Deanie Pass*.

Detail of "As Snug As A Bug In A Rug." *Courtesy of Deanie Pass*.

"The Muse Speaks." Sculptress turned rug hooker depicts a past life. Torn wool on linen with a braided border. Deanie Pass. 1998. 35" x 46". *Courtesy of Deanie Pass.*

Sometimes you just don't feel like facing the world. "How Does My Garden Grow." Torn wool strips on linen. Deanie Pass. 1999. 27" x 47". *Courtesy of Deanie Pass.*

"Behind The Scene" was made for a friend who, while not photographing lush tropical plants, knits incredible sweaters. The friend got the rug and Deanie got a sweater. Deanie Pass. 1999. 30" x 41". Commissioned by Stephanie Torbert. *Courtesy of Deanie Pass.*

What a magical way to travel the cities of Europe. "Camille's Magic Carpet / Le Tapis Volant De Camille." Torn wool strips on linen. Deanie Pass. 1999. 42" x 40". Gift to Camille Pass. *Courtesy of Deanie Pass.*

Champagne and sentiments are "Bubbling Over" in a big way in this small study. Deanie Pass. 2000. 10" x 10". Collection of Anna and Steve Carlson. *Courtesy of Deanie Pass*

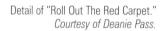

A special guest is arriving so "Roll Out The Red Carpet." Torn wool on linen. Deanie Pass. 2000. 38" x 65". *Courtesy of Deanie Pass.*

Detail of "Roll Out The Red Carpet." *Courtesy of Deanie Pass.*

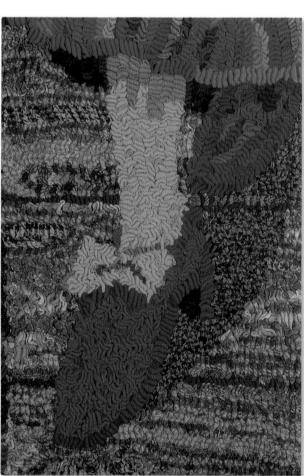

All artists seek inspiration from other artists. And Deanie Pass is no exception. "I Thought I Was Monet." Torn wool strips on linen with braided border. Deanie Pass. 2000. 33" x 38". *Courtesy of Deanie Pass.*

"Someone's In The Kitchen With Dinah" cooking up eggs and pie. Torn wool strips on linen with machine cut strips for lettering. Deanie Pass. 2000. 34" x 42". *Courtesy of Deanie Pass.*

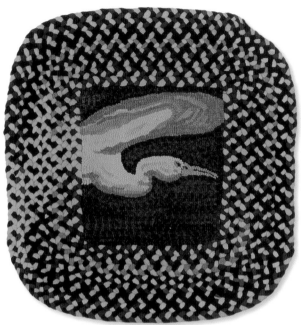

A limited palette was used in this portrait of "Stork For 2000." Machine cut wool on cotton with braided border. Deanie Pass. 2000. 24" x 24". Collection of Zack Pass. *Courtesy of Deanie Pass.*

Every housewife performs a "Balancing Act" on a daily basis but often without the applause. Torn wool on linen. Deanie Pass. 2000. 42" x 40". *Courtesy of Deanie Pass*

"For A Moment I Thought I Was Modigliani's Model" is the start of a new series in which Deanie trades places with historically recognizable women. Deanie Pass. 2001. 41" x 30". Collection of Patty Yoder. *Courtesy of Deanie Pass.*

"Friends Surround You – Family Does Too." We should all have such good fortune. Torn wool strips with braided edge. Deanie Pass. 2001. 36" x 36". Commissioned by Lois Spector. *Courtesy of Deanie Pass.*

A hooked rug becomes the canvas for "Let's Cut A Rug." Torn wool strips on linen with machine cut strips for lettering. Deanie Pass. 2002. 47" x 55". *Courtesy of Deanie Pass.*

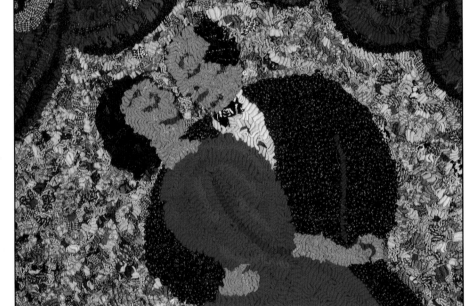

Detail of "Let's Cut A Rug." *Courtesy of Deanie Pass.*

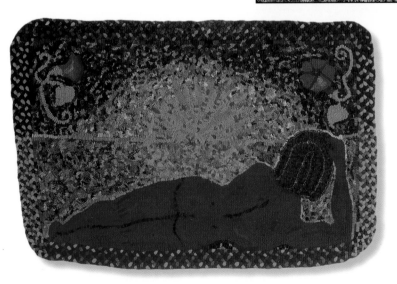

Take time to appreciate the "Morning Gloria." Torn wool on linen with braided edge. Deanie Pass. 2002. 30" x 45". *Courtesy of Deanie Pass.*

Emily K. Robertson, Falmouth, Massachusetts

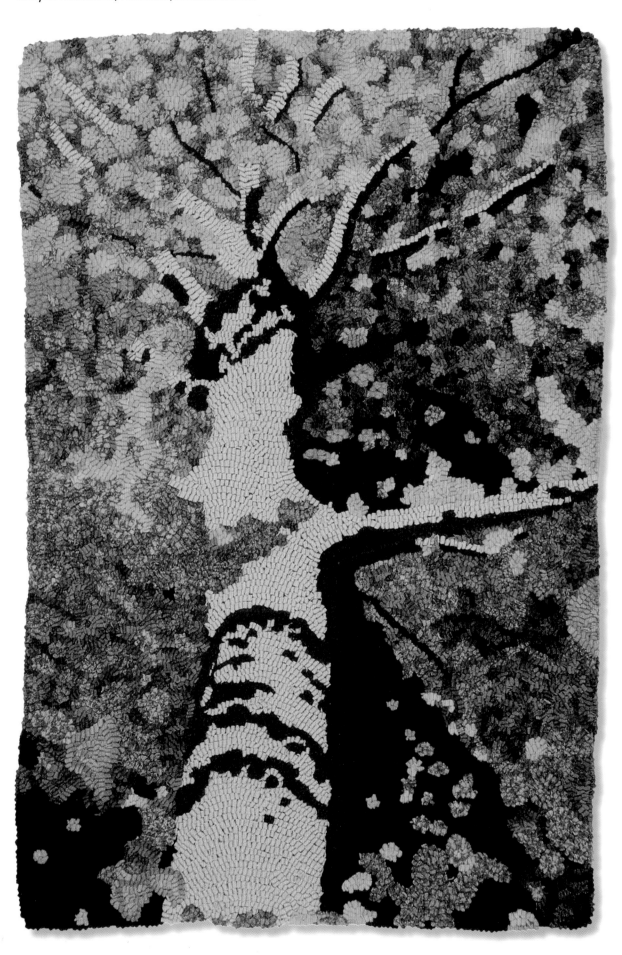

Illuminating and vibrant "Spring Comes To Elm Road" was inspired by a neighbor's tree. Emily Robertson. 2002. 26" x 18". Private Collection. *Courtesy of Emily Robertson.*

Rug hooking became part of my life when I decided to return to a creative life after a career in academic administration. I found rug hooking as a medium by going to the library and researching various crafts. The technique of traditional rug hooking fitted my abilities and time constraints. Since I had had substantial training in the arts I taught myself the basics of the craft. I soon made contact with local rug hooking groups and with rug camps. As I began hooking I thought I would have a primitive style and emulate a folk art approach. However, I soon found myself gravitating away from primitive images to a more painterly pictorial approach. Hooking was my medium, but I wanted to find my own style and to listen to my own muse. Light and shadow has and still does intrigue me and I love to take on the challenge of trying to do something new within the constraints of the craft.

I have been fortunate to be self-taught and to not have learned how to hook a rose or other image as some one else does or as tradition dictates. I do not think about the individual areas of my pieces, but rather concentrate on the overall image I am trying to convey. That is to say, I am not interested in making a rose within the context of the whole scene.

It does not bother me to part with my work when I have finished making it. I was an art major in college and was taught that if you were not able to tear up your very best drawings then you didn't belong in art. Artists are always improving and are confident of their talent. I have not yet made my best rug. I am not interested in looking at past projects. I'm interested in the next challenge. Doing commission work has been very satisfying to me because the client presents me with certain expectations and limitations and I love working within fixed perimeters to create a work of beauty and durability.

The ambiance of a Cape Cod summer is realized in this hooked portrayal of "Swing Lane, Falmouth, MA." Emily Robertson. 1999. 32" x 46". *Courtesy of Emily Robertson.*

"Window on Spring" captures a view from an art gallery in Wisconsin, Emily's former home state. Emily Robertson. 1997. 63" x 36". *Courtesy of Emily Robertson.*

"The Homestead" evokes over one hundred years of cherished family memories. Emily Robertson. 1997. 31" x 40". Collection of Dean Erickson. *Courtesy of Emily Robertson.*

Offering another view of "The Homestead" is "Katy and Dean's Home." Emily Robertson. 2000. 38" x 41". Collection of Dean Erickson. *Courtesy of Emily Robertson.*

"Chelsea Garden" captures the interplay of light and shadow found in a quiet corner of New York City. Emily Robertson. 1996. 54" x 38". *Courtesy of Emily Robertson.*

Emily Robertson's hooked art delights an international audience. Award winning, her work has been displayed in museums, galleries, and shows throughout the United States and in England and Japan as well as gracing numerous private collections. In addition to selling completed rugs she is willing to do commissioned work. Emily also teaches rug hooking.

A bit of old England graces this Wisconsin home. "Tudor Garden." Emily Robertson. 1997. 46" x 49". *Courtesy of Emily Robertson.*

"Grandma, Mammy, and Cousin Tom" pose at their home prior to a much anticipated visit to the 1893 Chicago World's Fair. Emily Robertson. 2000. 30" x 34". *Courtesy of Emily Robertson.*

Marking the occasion of opening a cottage for the upcoming summer season, "Up North" depicts a special Wisconsin vacation home. Emily Robertson. 1997. 40" x 49". *Courtesy of Emily Robertson.*

Strips cut from a plaid skirt and hooked to represent a field of wild flowers, surround a "Mother With Children" as they gather bouquets. This work is a portrait of the artist and her son and daughter. Emily Robertson. 1995. 34" x 29". Collection of the University of Wisconsin – Madison. *Courtesy of Emily Robertson.*

A vivid "Color Spectrum" forms the backdrop for a collection of pithy sayings. Emily Robertson. 2002. 44" x 46". Collection of Rae Reynolds Harrell. *Courtesy of Emily Robertson.*

Linda Rae Coughlin, Warren, New Jersey

My current body of work looks at women and the issues that pertain to their lives. Each piece is a narrative, pictorial essay that tells a story. When viewed, the work says many things on many levels by using color, texture, shapes, symbols, and words. Being in touch with the energy that flows around us all, it is my goal that when viewed my work will elicit an emotional response.

"Strength-Hope-Liberty" was commissioned by the New Jersey Cancer Research Society shortly after September 11, 2001 to honor American patriotism. Linda Rae Coughlin. 2002. 30" x 20". *Courtesy of Linda Rae Coughlin.*

"Obstacles." In the artist's own words, "Our blessings come in many packages." Linda Rae Coughlin. 2001. 40" x 30". *Courtesy of Linda Rae Coughlin.*

"Men-O-Pause" brings to light a natural but little discussed passage in every women's life. Linda Rae Coughlin. 2001. 54" x 22". *Courtesy of Linda Rae Coughlin.*

The elements of earth, air, fire, and water combine with the human spirit in "Standing Naked." Linda Rae Coughlin. 1999. 48" x 28". *Courtesy of Linda Rae Coughlin.*

"Merrily, Merrily, Merrily, Werrily, Life Is But a Dream" was inspired by the children's song, "Row, Row, Row Your Boat." Linda Rae Coughlin. 1999. 28" x 34". *Courtesy of Linda Rae Coughlin.*

"No Braver Soul Than I" pays tribute to all women who have undergone cancer treatment. Linda Rae Coughlin. 1999. 23" x 20". *Courtesy of Linda Rae Coughlin.*

A whimsical children's song was the force behind "Worms." Linda Rae Couglin. 1998. 31" x 36". *Courtesy of Linda Rae Coughlin.*

Linda Rae's thought provoking work is available from the artist and selected galleries. Plans for the future include curating a traveling exposition of hooked pieces that highlight all aspects of playing cards.

"Oh Honey" is dedicated to women who find that their husbands just don't listen. Linda Rae Coughlin. 1997. 33" x 33". *Courtesy of Linda Rae Coughlin.*

"The Blues" reminds us all to be grateful for what we have. Linda Rae Couglin. 1997. 36" x 48". *Courtesy of Linda Rae Coughlin.*

Inspired by an antique hooked rug created to honor the dead, Linda Rae Coughlin has planned for the inevitable with "My Ropes - If I Can't Break My Ropes Now, Do I Really Expect To Do It Later." It is the artist's wish that this, her own funeral rug, not be put to use for many years to come. Linda Rae Coughlin. 1997. 28" x 38". *Courtesy of Linda Rae Coughlin.*

Chapter Four

Tools of the Trade

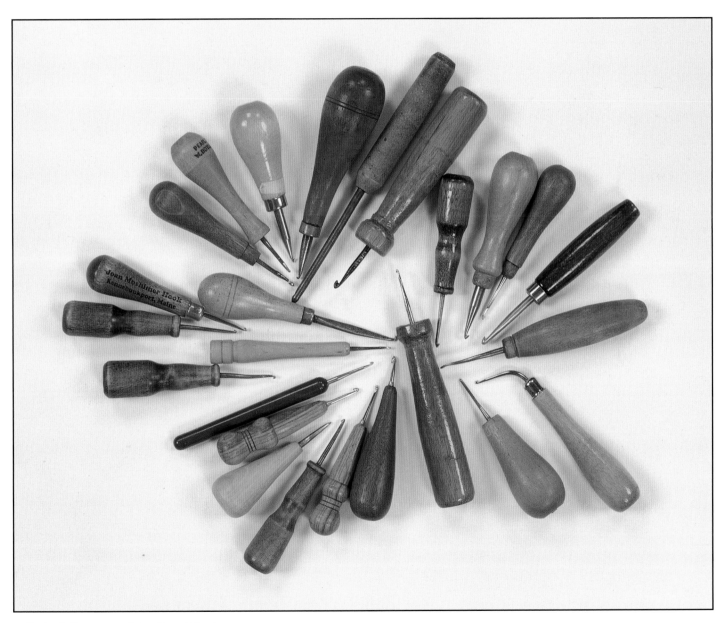

Hooks of all ages are an interesting addition to your rug
collection and generally cost under $10.

The tools of the hooking trade such as old hooks, cutters, patterns, frames, and books make an interesting addition to your rug collection. Knowing what you're buying can be to your advantage. Rug making hooks are at times incorrectly labeled as button hooks for shoes, and cutters, used to slice strips of wool, are sold as pasta makers. Collectors are always in search of books, magazines, auction catalogs, or anything related to rug hooking. Prices reflect the growing interest but bargains can be found.

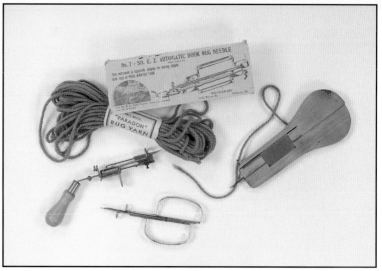

Shuttle hooks, punch hooks, and hook rug needles were made primarily for use with yarns but could also accommodate strips of fabric.

Hand-cranked cutters, used to slice woolen fabric into strips as thin as 2/32 of an inch wide, have been popular with rug hookers since the 1930s. Many have interchangeable cutting wheels.

Rug hookers and collectors will buy anything written about their favorite subject.

Old rug hooking patterns are often mounted and hung on the wall as is. Hooking the pattern is not a good idea. Doing so would drastically reduce any antique value. E.S. Frost & Co., Biddeford, Maine. 1870-1890.

Another fine example of an old hooked rug pattern. Ralph Burnham's Patterns on Burlap. No. 61. Ipswich, Massachusetts. 1920-1930. From the Ralph Burnham Collection.

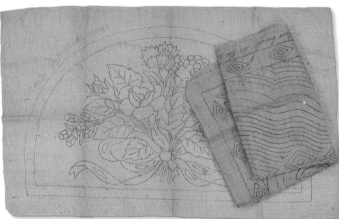

Rug hooking patterns reflect popular decorating trends. Those that are in poor condition are of little monetary value. They are too fragile to hook and should be used for display purposes only.

Partially completed hooked rugs are no bargain no matter how inexpensively priced. Often the burlap foundation is in poor condition and the fabrics needed to finish the job are long gone.

Old wooden hooking frames are rarely used by today's rug makers. They were heavy, cumbersome, and did not allow the hooker to view the entire rug. As work progressed the finished portion of the rug was rolled up and out of sight. Often inexpensively priced or given away. Those handmade from exotic woods are of more interest to collectors. Early 20th century.

Chapter Five
Where to Find Antique and Collectible Hooked Rugs

It may take a little searching but old hooked rugs can be found in a variety of places.

The antique trade papers are a must for all collectors. Available by subscription or through some antique shops and newspaper stands, these weekly, biweekly, and monthly publications list upcoming auctions, flea markets, and shows as well as advertising shops and individual dealers. Some focus on local happenings. Others offer a nationwide calendar of what's going on and what's being sold. They also contain interesting articles about auctions, popular shows, collections, collectors, and the going prices of everything from wooden apples to zithers.

Magazines that feature antiques or collectibles can also be a good source of information.

SHOPS

Visiting antique, co-op, and second hand shops on a regular basis is a good way to start your search for hooked rugs. Establish a relationship with the shop's owner and stop by often. Let it be known what type of hooked rug you're looking for and what you can afford.

Antique shops offer a wide array of merchandise including hooked rugs. *Courtesy of Jane C. Blanchard, Jeremiah Dalton House Antiques, Wiscasset, Maine.*

Hooked rugs lend color and warmth to any décor. *Courtesy of Jane C. Blanchard, Jeremiah Dalton House Antiques, Wiscasset, Maine.*

SHOWS AND FLEA MARKETS

Antique shows and flea markets bring together a wide variety of dealers from many different locations. At these events expect to see hooked rugs of varying age, style, size, condition, and price. If you are lucky you might even find a dealer who specializes in what you're looking for. If not, ask around as to who sells hooked rugs. Someone will surely give you a name or lead to follow.

Hooked, braided, and needlework rugs complement country furnishings. RJG Antiques at Heart of the Country Antiques Show, Nashville, Tennessee, March 2001. *Courtesy of Russ and Karen Goldberger / RJG Antiques, Rye, New Hampshire.*

Antique hooked rugs depicting animals are much in demand. This primitive portrayal of twin rearing horses possesses the naive qualities that folk art collectors covet. RJG Antiques at Jim Burk's York, Pennsylvania Antiques Show. May 2001. *Courtesy of Russ and Karen Goldberger / RJG Antiques, Rye, New Hampshire.*

Brimfield

Three times a year thousands of dealers from across the United States, Canada, and beyond converge on the small central Massachusetts town of Brimfield to buy, sell, and trade their wares during a much anticipated week long extravaganza. Held in May, July, and September, the Brimfield Flea Market has attracted millions of collectors since antique dealer Gordon Reid started the show in 1959.

The sun had barely risen the May morning in 1999 when I took these photographs. Buyers were out and about and in serious pursuit of desired objects. For many, including myself, going to Brimfield is a tradition; one that no collector should miss.

Offered at the Hawks Nest Antiques booth was this exceptional Grenfell mat of ducks in flight, hooked in the early 1900s at the Grenfell Labrador Industries. Brimfield Flea Market. *Courtesy of Hawks Nest Antiques, Hinesburg, Vermont.*

The Brimfield Flea Market is a collector's paradise. Hooked rugs of every age, size, and design vie for the attention of eager early morning shoppers. *Courtesy of Hawks Nest Antiques, Hinesburg, Vermont.*

Floral hooked rugs were to be found among the eclectic treasures at this Brimfield Flea Market booth. *Courtesy of Jan Hale, Corn Crib Antiques, Henniker, New Hampshire.*

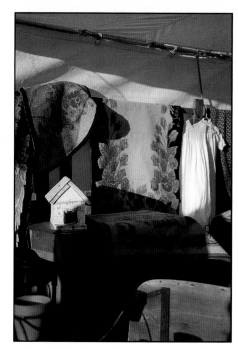

Geometric design hooked rugs are always popular and complement both antique and contemporary interiors. Brimfield Flea Market. *Courtesy of Highfields Antiques, St. Albans, Maine.*

Corn Crib Antiques offered hooked rugs with roses; both realistic and fanciful. Brimfield Flea Market. *Courtesy of Jan Hale, Corn Crib Antiques, Henniker, New Hampshire.*

Testing out the product. Brimfield Flea Market. *Courtesy of Highfields Antiques, St. Albans, Maine.*

An early morning shopper tries to make a decision. By the end of the day this booth was bare. Brimfield Flea Market. *Courtesy of Susan Page, Lincoln, Massachusetts.*

Room-sized hand-hooked rugs in good condition such as this one of floral and scroll design are few and far between. Brimfield Flea Market. *Courtesy of Susan Page, Lincoln, Massachusetts.*

A vintage bath tub holds a variety of floor coverings including a 1940s striped block design hooked rug. Brimfield Flea Market. *Courtesy of Jeff R. Bridgman Antiques, Mansfield, Pennsylvania.*

ESTATE SALES AND YARD SALES

Check out estate sales and yard or tag sales. You never know what you might find. Most local newspapers offer listings of upcoming sales.

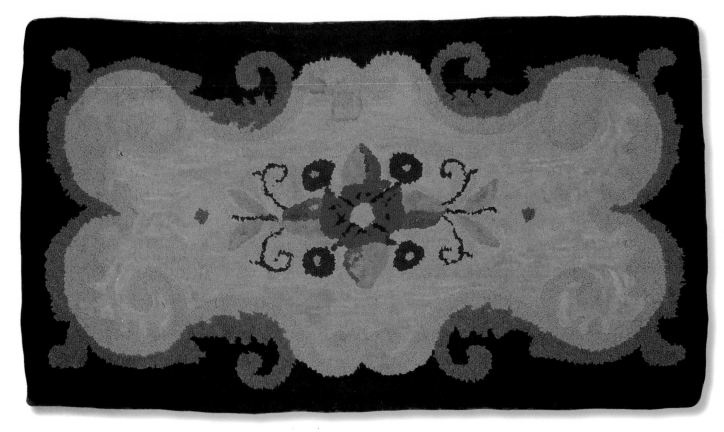

A yard sale find. An unpretentious hand-hooked rug in good condition and priced at $5. 1940-1960. 21" x 37".

AUCTIONS

Auctions are very popular with both dealers and collectors. The antique trade papers offer the most extensive and complete listing of what's being sold and where. Regional newspapers advertise local auctions. Some auction houses routinely mail out flyers or catalogs and if requested will send a follow- up list of realized prices. There generally is a charge for auction catalogs. Often filled with color photographs and detailed descriptions, these catalogs are a joy to look through, helpful at time of bidding, and an excellent reference source for future acquisitions. An all hooked rug auction is an infrequent event. When they happen, and they do, the auctioneer is guaranteed a full house and spirited bidding. Realistically if hooked rugs are being offered you can expect to find three or four of varying age, style, size, and condition. Make sure you attend the preview and carefully examine what you're bidding on. If unable to attend, some auctioneers, with pre-approval, will accept absentee bids. Auction prices for hooked rugs can range from a few dollars up to tens of thousands of dollars.

On August 5, 2000 Northeast Auctions of Portsmouth, New Hampshire offered for sale the Americana collection of Virginia Ramsey-Pope Cave, a noted New England antiques dealer, collector, and benefactress to New York's Museum of American Folk Art. Included were more than 400 lots of American country painted and formal furniture, folk art including paintings and sculptures, game boards and toys, hooked rugs and quilted coverlets, and decorative accessories. An eager audience awaited and bidding was spirited. With permission Northeast Auctions has kindly allowed me to reprint a sampling of the many fine hooked rugs offered, their auction catalog descriptions, and the prices realized. Prices do not include the buyer's premium.

NORTHEAST AUCTIONS
Saturday, August 5th, 2000
Manchester, New Hampshire

AMERICANA COLLECTION OF
VIRGINIA RAMSEY-POPE CAVE

The catalog cover chosen by Northeast Auctions for a much anticipated sale of Americana depicts a close-up of one of the many hooked rugs that were offered. The centennial rug was the subject of spirited bidding and proved to be a "star" of the show. *Courtesy of Northeast Auctions, Portsmouth, New Hampshire.*

American floral hooked rug. The central basket of colorful flowers on tan ground within lunette surround enclosing floral devices, the blue striped borders with floral spandrel corners. 36" x 63". Sold for $1,500. *Courtesy of Northeast Auctions, Portsmouth, New Hampshire*.

American hooked rug depicting an Indian brave. The full-length figure has a feathered headdress, a navy blue shirt with tan bandoleer, and camel pants with red belt, and is holding a walking stick, all on striated cream ground with grass. Mounted on black cloth and stretcher. 36" x 18". Provenance Billy Pearson Collection; David A. Schorsch. Sold for $8,500. *Courtesy of Northeast Auctions, Portsmouth, New Hampshire*.

Home-Sweet-Home hooked rug. Centering a house with chimney with flanking birds in trees, dog, and large rabbit, within camel and gray-green borders, in white, yellow, blue yarns. Mounted on stretcher. 30.5" x 61". Provenance: David Wheatcroft. Sold for $5,500. Hooked runner with floral motif. The striated black, brown, and cream ground with rose-red flower heads and leafage. 4' x 12'. Provenance: Anita Swatkowsky. Sold for $7,500. *Courtesy of Northeast Auctions, Portsmouth, New Hampshire*.

Hooked rug with checkerboard design and stylized birds. The alternating red and blue-gray blocks with multicolor striated border with abstract motifs and colorful bird in each corner. Mounted on stretcher. 28.5" x 43". Sold for $16,000. *Courtesy of Northeast Auctions, Portsmouth, New Hampshire*.

Room-size hooked rug with overall polychrome floral design. The cream ground with central floral vignette and floral corner spandrels enclosed by wide inner border with stylized vine and narrow brown-black outer border. 9' x 12'. Sold for $17,500. *Courtesy of Northeast Auctions Portsmouth, New Hampshire.*

American or Canadian hooked rug depicting dog. The dog worked in tan yarns with decorative black collar within colorful abstract background with blue scallops and striped candy canes. 27.5" x 39.5". Provenance: Stephen Score. Est. $6,000-$8,000. Sold for $31,000. *Courtesy of Northeast Auctions, Portsmouth, New Hampshire.*

Hooked rug with red horse and cow. On sage green ground with leafy branches in tan yarns, the sides with blue fringe border, mounted on stretcher. 25" x 39". Sold for $1,400. Hooked and sewn floral rug. With central wreath of red roses on slate blue ground and four floral spandrels in scrolls on dark gray ground. 50" x 85". Provenance: Sotheby's, June 1998, lot 1140. Sold for $5,500. *Courtesy of Northeast Auctions, Portsmouth, New Hampshire.*

Hooked rug with floral design. The cream ground with red and purple floral sprays alternating with apple green fronds and foliage within black border. 26" x 59". Sold for $500. *Courtesy of Northeast Auctions, Portsmouth, New Hampshire.*

Graphic squares hooked rug. The twelve boxes of concentric squares worked in yellow, red, pink, blue, gray, and green. Mounted on stretcher. 28.5" x 40". Provenance: Paula Rubenstein. Sold for $1,250. *Courtesy of Northeast Auctions, Portsmouth, New Hampshire.*

The cherry pickers hooked and tufted rug. Depicting two young girls and their dog amidst flowers and cherries on branches on black ground. Mounted on stretcher. 24" x 38". Provenance: Sotheby's, January 1998, lot 1468. Sold for $4,000. Floral geometric hooked runner. The floral sprigs within shaped ovals with concentric borders in browns, pinks, and greens, one oval signed "Mattie." 4' x 12'. Provenance: Anita Swatowsky. Sold for $2,000. *Courtesy of Northeast Auctions, Portsmouth, New Hampshire.*

American pictorial hooked rug "Talk To Me." Depicting facing roosters within a meandering trellis and vine border, worked with colorful yarns with pinks and blues predominant on gray ground. 32.5" x 44" Provenance: Stephen Score. Sold for $5,000. American hooked rug with three stars. With colorful abstract animal and floral motifs on striated ground within sawtooth border. 34" x 78". Sold for $6,000. *Courtesy of Northeast Auctions, Portsmouth, New Hampshire.*

Unusual American stars and stripes variation pattern hooked rug in red, white, and blue. The central five-point star within concentric diamonds and squares with stars with stripes overall in striated red, white, and blue. According to tradition, this rug was made from strips of old flags. 54" x 50.5". Provenance: This rug appears in a photograph in the SPNEA (Society for the Preservation of New England Antiquities) archives of the Parlor at Indian Hill, West Newbury, Massachusetts. It was probably taken at the turn of the century. Stephen Score. Literature: For information about Indian Hill, home of Ben: Perley Poore (1820-1887) see Elizabeth Stillinger's *The Antiquers*, pp. 27- 33. Poore's daughter married Frederick Strong Mosley. Est. $7,500-9,500. Sold for $40,000. *Courtesy of Northeast Auctions, Portsmouth, New Hampshire.*

American hooked rug with facing rabbits and bouquet of flowers dated 1892. The rabbits worked in shades of cream centering a large ribboned bouquet with red, pink, white, and blue flowers on striated camel ground below camel and navy yarns with floral spray corner spandrels. The date within multiple borders of pink, cream, rose, and camel stripes. 28" x 48". Provenance: Stella Rubin. Sold for $12,000. *Courtesy of Northeast Auctions, Portsmouth, New Hampshire.*

BUYING ON-LINE

You can also buy hooked rugs on the Internet, utilizing on-line auctions such as eBay. Using this method can be fun and educational. Some rugs are correctly dated and condition accurately reported. Good quality hooked rugs at bargain prices can be found. But a common problem is that many machine-made hooked rugs are incorrectly described as hand-hooked. The true ages of the rugs can be exaggerated and their condition enhanced. Foundation dry rot or the displeasing smell of animal urine cannot be realized on a computer screen. Make sure any rugs purchased on-line can be returned if you are not completely satisfied.

INHERITED GIFTS

I am the family wardrobe, best and worst
Of all generations, from the first;
Grandpa's Sunday-go-to-meetin' coat,
And the woollen muffler he wore at his throat;
Grandma's shawl, that came from Fayal:
Ma's wedding gown, three times turned
*   and once let, down,*
Which once was plum but now turned brown;
Pa's red flannels that made him itch;
Pants and shirts; petticoats and skirts;
From one or another, but I can't tell which.
Tread carefully, because you see, if you scuff me,
You scratch the bark of the family tree.[1]

—Nineteenth Century Canadian Rug Rhyme

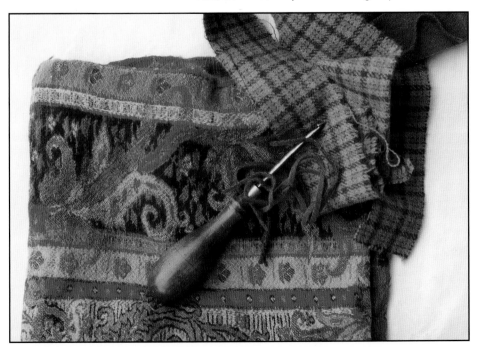

Most cherished are those rugs hooked from the cut up clothing of loved ones.

Hooked rugs are often inherited by family members or given to others who appreciate handwork. Rug hookers, family members of rug hookers, and collectors want their hooked possessions with those who share their passion. These rugs often come with interesting stories of where and why they were made or how they were acquired. This information should be recorded and passed along to the next generation of admirers.

The Collection of Samuel and Susan Keith: A Mother's Legacy

Susan Keith shares her mother-in-law's story.

Goldie Keith's interest in rug hooking began in the late 1950s when she wanted something to add to her needle crafts of sewing and knitting. She found a talented teacher in Lenox, Massachusetts named Sally Newhall, one of Pearl McGown's students, and began the monthly daylong sessions at Ms Newhall's studio. Thus begins a process that her son remembers vividly. Walking into a home with wet wool boiling on the stove and the smell of vinegar and all sorts of other unfamiliar odors became a frequent occurrence. Initially working with a hand-cranked cutter (looking like the contemporary pasta maker) his mother would cut the now dry wool into thin strips. The first casualties were his father's old blue navy uniforms, which formed the background for a floral oval design now centered under the family dining table. But, ul-

A series of twelve stained glass windows representing the Twelve Tribes of Israel created in 1962 by Russian born painter Marc Chagall (1887-1985) inspired Goldie Keith's hooked version of "The Jerusalem Windows." 1978. 76" x 52.5". *Courtesy of Susan and Samuel Keith.*

This abstract study reveals Mrs. Keith's fascination with the interaction of color and shape. Hooked between the late 1970s and the early 1990s. 44" x 33". *Courtesy of Susan and Samuel Keith.*

timately the most available pieces of wool were used up and Mrs. Keith turned to a new source.

Sitting alphabetically next to her son in boarding school was a young man whose father owned a cashmere mill in Connecticut. After hearing of this in a conversation about school, Mrs. Keith asked her son to find out what the mill did with their "mill-ends" and if they were for sale. From that point on, Mrs. Keith purchased large quantities of the bulk "mill-ends" which in their natural state were a perfect off-white color ideally suitable for dyeing. Initially she made rugs from patterns. Then, she began creating her own designs that were often natural subjects such as leaves, seashells, and butterflies.

In the late 1970s she made a rug of Marc Chagall's "Jerusalem Windows." In 1962 Chagall created a series of twelve stained glass windows representing the Twelve Tribes of Israel. The "Jerusalem Windows" had two elements that were critical to her later work. First, according to one source, the essence of the windows lies in color. "Chagall's palette is inexhaustible, quick in sharp or subtle contrasts and it can enliven with infinite nuances a vast expanse dominated by a single color."[2] Since Chagall was forbidden to depict the human form in them, the windows possess a many-layered symbolism. "Rather than tending toward decorative and picturesque representation, the absence of the human figure gives majestic and universal resonance to the purity of the fundamental symbols."[3]

Having been liberated from traditional forms, her work began to focus more on color and its ability to communicate an impression, such as her work which portrays a sunset without any representative references. It is not surprising that in the 1980s her attention was drawn to the work of Wassily Kandinsky. From then until her death in May 1999, she concentrated on his art and translated it into her creations. Early in his work, Kandinsky had searched for ways to eliminate traditional representation in art. Kandinsky's work conveys the artist's emotional response to events of an internal nature. That feeling is a result of a combination of experiences; on one hand those perceptions that arise from the artist's inner world, on the other, the impressions the artist receives from external appearances, events, or concepts. "Kandinsky assigned much greater evocative power to color than to form. He acknowledged, however, that color and form are the fundamental vehicles of content in painting and Kandinsky's primary aim was to achieve the ultimate harmony of these means in a way that would best reflect the beauty of inner feeling, the beauty of the new spiritual."[4] Mrs. Keith often expressed that, by translating his work, she felt she had gotten inside Kandinsky's head.

Beginning in the 1980s and up until her death in 1999 Goldie Keith concentrated on the work of Russian-born painter Wassily Kandinsky (1866-1944). With strips of woolen fabric she translated the artist's colorful brush strokes into her own hooked work. 1993. 33.5" x 57". *Courtesy of Susan and Samuel Keith.*

A bold and bright yellow plane floats above a somber field in Goldie Keith's Kandinsky-inspired hooked painting. 1993. 33.5" x 57". *Courtesy of Susan and Samuel Keith.*

Goldie Keith captured a feeling of ongoing motion in this Kandinsky-inspired abstract. 1980s. 69.5" x 45.5". *Courtesy of Susan and Samuel Keith.*

Top right: Kandinsky's unrestrained use of color, combined with a collection of playful shapes, intrigued and motivated Mrs. Keith. 1980s. 44" x 57.5". *Courtesy of Susan and Samuel Keith.*

Center right: Another of Goldie Keith's early hooked Kandinsky studies. 1980s. 36.5" x 59". *Courtesy of Susan and Samuel Keith.*

Bursting with life; a hooked geometric Kandinsky. Goldie Keith. 1980s-1990s. 45.5" x 69.5". *Courtesy of Susan and Samuel Keith.*

Made with love to honor a member of the Freemasons. A variety of fabrics, including a paisley shawl were cut into strips and then hooked into this Frost pattern. From the Ralph Burnham Collection. 1880-1900. 24" x 36".

Ralph Burnham, "the Hooked Rug Magnate" of Ipswich, Massachusetts, advertised an inventory of over three thousand rugs and was responsible during the early 1900s for carpeting some of America's most elegant homes. Through the kindness and generosity of his niece, rug hooking artist and teacher Annie Spring, the Masonic design hooked rug that once hung in Burnham's studio now hangs in mine.

In 1905 Ipswich, Massachusetts antique dealer Ralph Burnham advertised an inventory of over 3,000 hooked rugs. For those who wished to create their own he sold preprinted patterns. *Courtesy of Annie A. Spring.*

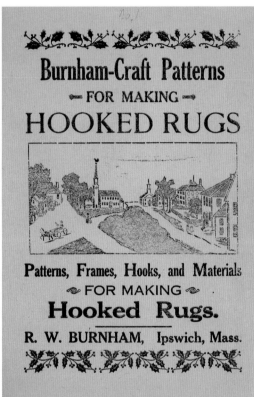

Ralph Burham's able staff worked six days a week making and repairing hooked rugs. The half round rug with the Masonic emblem hanging from the rafters now graces my studio. *Courtesy of Annie A. Spring.*

A Closer Look At Gardner King's Hooked Rugs

Nothing made Gardner King (1893-1963) happier than to be hooking rugs with his daughter Rosie by his side. From his Fitchburg, Massachusetts home, the talented Mr. King crafted an impressive number of rugs utilizing many of his own designs. Years later due to Rosie's love and determination the collection of her beloved father's work remains intact. A close-up look follows.

Utilizing both preprinted patterns and designs of his own, Gardner King hooked from the mid 1930s until his death in 1963. A close-up look at details from a variety of his scenic rugs reveals his preference for using a wide range of color. *Courtesy of Rosalie Lent.*

Floral motifs were bright and cheerful. Gardner King. *Courtesy of Rosalie Lent*.

Backgrounds were never dull. Gardner King. *Courtesy of Rosalie Lent*.

UNLIKELY PLACES

One man's trash can be another man's treasure. Several hooked rugs in my collection are rescued finds from a local town dump. Some I hauled out of dumpsters. Others were snatched away from piles of trash left at the side of the road for pick up. Be cautious when acquiring rugs of questionable background. Examine carefully. The price may be right but not if it means putting the rest of your hooked rug collection at risk.

Clean, in good condition, and rescued from the town dump. Not an exceptional hooked rug but charming in simplicity of color and design. The rug maker attempted to replicate traditional floral and scroll patterns but fell naively short of the goal. 1930-1950. 20" x 34".

Chapter Six

Where to Find New Hooked Rugs

She may not sell her work but June Mikoryak unselfishly shares her joy of rug hooking. For over 10 years the beloved Michigan rug hooking teacher has encouraged and guided some of today's finest hooking artists. June's award winning "Bicentennial Eagle" rug, adapted from an early Frost pattern includes an original background scene of a picturesque New England village. It was the second rug she hooked. 1976. 32" x 65". *Courtesy of June Mikoryak*.

Located in Montpelier, Vermont, Green Mountain Hooked Rugs, Inc., offers supplies, classes, week long workshops, and new and used hooked rugs. Pictured are three generations of the rug hooking Ashworth family, Wink Ashworth, Stephanie Ashworth Krauss, and Cecely Conrad. *Courtesy of Stephanie Ashworth Krauss*.

Hooking is a popular craft. Just about everybody knows or has heard of someone who hooks rugs. The heaviest concentration of enthusiasts is in the United States and Canada, with growing numbers around the globe. Information about these groups, as well as rug hooking in general, is available on-line and in rug hooking newsletters and magazines and through suppliers. Inquire at a school or college that offers adult education courses or at your local library or community center as to where you might find a rug hooking teacher or hooking group. It may take a little searching but your efforts will be rewarded. Rug hookers tend to be very friendly and love to share their zest for what often is a lifelong passion. Some will sell their work. But be aware that for many selling a rug is like selling a child.

Since undertaking this project many of those who would never part with their rugs have reconsidered. And as I was told by a very wise rug hooker, "Everything has a price."

Many old rugs are the inspiration for new rugs. Burnham's 1938 catalog offered this burlap pattern, "No. 88 - 40" x 100" - Early American Geometrical" for $2.50. A rug of similar design can be found at the Beauport-Sleeper, McCann House in Gloucester, Massachusetts, a property belonging to the Society for the Preservation of New England Antiquities. "Beauport Geometric." June Robbs. 2001. 34" x 58". *Courtesy of June Robbs.*

What follows is a sampling of those who truly love to hook and are willing to sell their work.

Rae Reynolds Harrell, Hinesburg, Vermont

Eve tempts Adam with "The Apple" as God watches over the scene. Note the rug's scalloped border. Rae Reynolds Harrell. 2000. 34" x 33". *Courtesy of Rae Reynolds Harrell.*

Art has been one of the most gratifying areas of my life, as it has always brought me joy. I have worked in many mediums and love them all, but rug hooking is on the top of the list. There is a meditative quality to the act of hooking, i.e., the quiet motion and the resultant image of the finished product. I approach this skill as creative art and the linen or monk's cloth backing as my canvas. I do not use patterns but work from my inner creative resources. Usually, I have an idea sketched in the center of my backing and then allow the rest to evolve in a natural uninhibited flow. As the image unravels, I can sit back and enjoy the emotional fulfillment it gives me.

I teach rug hooking and try to incorporate the philosophy of using time to grow as a human being. My home in Vermont provides tranquility for my classes and has created the setting in which many beautiful and inspired pieces of art have evolved. This is one of my proudest accomplishments.

That which none can avoid and all should embrace. "Time Brings Change and Growth." Designed by the artist's daughter, Rebecca Harrell and hooked by Rae Reynolds Harrell. 2000. 39" x 31". *Courtesy of Rae Reynolds Harrell.*

A view that no x-ray could ever reveal. "Only In My Mind." Rae Reynolds Harrell. 2002. 26" x 24". *Courtesy of Rae Reynolds Harrell.*

Some dream in satin and lace but "I Dream In Paisley." Rae Reynolds Harrell. 2001. 40" x 60". *Courtesy of Rae Reynolds Harrell.*

I Dream in Paisley

Rae Reynolds Harrell's work is available from the artist and can be seen at selected shows. She will also consider doing commissioned pieces.

Vibrant and illuminating, this blue moon dominates a collage of colors, shapes, designs, and textures. "Once In A Blue Moon." Rae Reynolds Harrell. 2001. 50" x 36". *Courtesy of Rae Reynolds Harrell.*

Trish Johnson – Fergus, Ontario, Canada

I want to hook rugs depicting places important to my family history. My happiest childhood memories are of summer vacations spent in New Brunswick. When life is too complicated, I like to think about my ancestors living on Grand Manan Island calling their kids into supper from their play along the shore among the wharves and fishing sheds.

Trish Johnson's great grandfather built, but never lived in "W. L. Harvey House." The ship builder turned lighthouse keeper sold the Grand Manan Island home to his brother-in-law for $500 but never received payment. Trish Johnson. 1996. 23" x 34". *Courtesy of Trish Johnson.*

Detail of "W. L. Harvey House." *Courtesy of Trish Johnson.*

Swallowtail Light is the first thing you see when approaching Grand Manan Island by ferry. Depicted is Trish's seven year old son, the same age as the artist when she first saw her ancestors' home. "Douglas At Swallowtail." Trish Johnson. 1997. 24" x 35.5". *Courtesy of Trish Johnson.*

Detail of "Douglas At Swallowtail." *Courtesy of Trish Johnson.*

"Gannet Rock" lighthouse in the Bay of Fundy was one of Trish's grandmother's childhood homes. Storms were once so fierce that rushing water forced the wood stove across the kitchen floor. Trish Johnson. 1998. 24" x 34". *Courtesy of Trish Johnson*.

Detail of "Gannet Rock." *Courtesy of Trish Johnson*.

Three generations of Trish's family, including herself, have lived in "Grandpa Johnson's House." Located in Capreol, Ontario, the house was built from two freight cars that were pushed up the hill from the Canadian National railroad yards. Trish Johnson. 1998. 23" x 33.5". *Courtesy of Trish Johnson.*

Tethered because there are no fences, "Baby Jean" grazes at the family farm in Jones Creek, New Brunswick. Trish Johnson. 2000. 30.5" x 20.5". *Courtesy of Trish Johnson.*

"My grandmother lived on Machias Seal island, where her father was the keeper of the light. She met Jim Balmer, the Captain of the schooner Clayola, when he was delivering coal. When he left she wrote in her diary 'and that ends the Clayola and Captain Balmer at Machias Seal Island.' Later she went back and corrected her entry; 'That does not end Captain Balmer at Machias Seal Island.' She married him and had three daughters, one of whom was my mother." "My Grandmother's Diary, 1911." Trish Johnson. 2002. 27" x 37". *Courtesy of Trish Johnson.*

Detail of "My Grandmother's Diary, 1911." *Courtesy of Trish Johnson.*

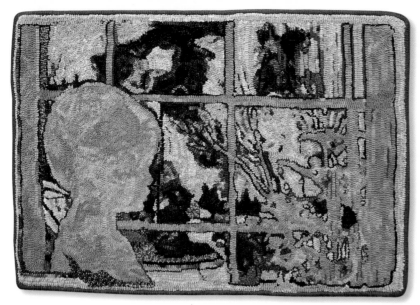

Photographer and hooking artist Trish Johnson is interested in doing commissioned work of people's childhood homes and also of their children's artwork. She embraces and preserves that which we hold dear.

A silhouette of the artist's son, "Patrick At Peachwillow Lane," was inspired by a black and white photo and a computer printer that was running out of ink. Trish Johnson. 1999. 23" x 33". *Courtesy of Trish Johnson.*

"Minuet One" recreates young Patrick's drawing and recalls many hours of enjoyment spent in the Suzuki violin program. Trish Johnson. 2000. 22.5" x 51.5". *Courtesy of Trish Johnson.*

Leonard Cohen wrote in *Suzanne*, "and she brings me tea and oranges that come all the way from China." Trish pays tribute to her grandmother who was always heading up to her room with a cup of tea and some orange sections on a saucer. "A Gift From Suzanne To Leonard." Trish Johnson. 2002. 9" x 9". *Courtesy of Trish Johnson.*

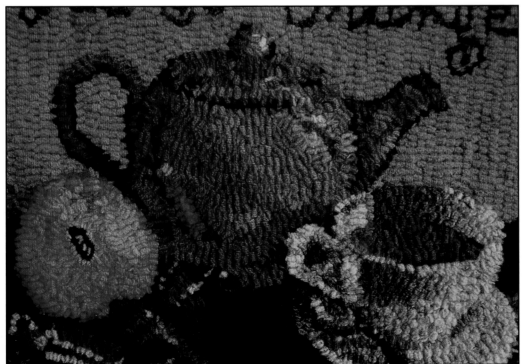

Detail of "A Gift From Suzanne To Leonard." *Courtesy of Trish Johnson.*

MUSEUMS AND GALLERIES

Due to the public's growing interest in hooked art an increasing number of museums, galleries, and shops are showing and selling hooked textiles. Exhibitions can feature the work of many or spot light just one or two artists. Prices reflect the artist's talent, credentials, and following.

Offer them hooked rugs and they will come. "Show and Tell." Susan Smidt. 2000. 24" x 36". *Courtesy of Susan Smidt.*

Opposite page, bottom: "Remembering When – Rug Hookers Reminisce" highlighted the talents of an international and select group of hooking artists. The three-month long exhibit attracted a record-breaking audience. Pat Merikallio's "Alexandra" hangs ready to greet visitors. Pat Merikallio. 1996. 52" x 42". *Courtesy of Wenham Museum, Wenham, Massachusetts.*

Wenham Museum

During the summer of 1998, the Wenham Museum in conjunction with the Association of Traditional Hooking Artists hosted a juried exhibition of contemporary hand-hooked rugs. To complement the exhibit the museum's 17th century Clafin-Richards House showcased a private collection of antique hooked rugs. *Courtesy of the Wenham Museum, Wenham, Massachusetts.*

During the summer of 1998 the Wenham Museum of Wenham, Massachusetts in conjunction with the Association of Traditional Hooking Artists (ATHA) sponsored a juried showing of contemporary hooked art. The much-anticipated event drew entries and visitors from throughout the United States, Canada, Europe, and Asia. To highlight rug hooking's glorious past the museum's historic Clafin-Richards House was filled with antique hooked rugs and related items. Some of the contemporary hooked art on exhibit was offered for sale.

A cherished childhood doll house, made for the Chamberlain sisters in the late 1880s by their father, a Massachusetts silversmith, and now a prized part of the Wenham Museum Collection, was the inspiration for this rug. Jeanie Crockett. 1998. 43" x 54". *Courtesy of Jeanie Crockett.*

Ralph Burnham, "Hooked Rug Magnate" and owner of the Ipswich, Massachusetts Antique Trading Post, advertised an inventory of over 3,000 rugs and was responsible for carpeting the homes of many notable clients including the du Ponts and Wanamakers during the early 1900s. Annie Spring, niece of the late Mr. Burnham, patterned "Burnham Floral" after the center motif of "Burnham Legacy," a rug originally hooked in the 1880s and displayed at the Metropolitan Museum of Fine Art in New York City. Annie A. Spring. 1990. 48" x 32". *Courtesy of Annie A. Spring and the Wenham Museum, Wenham, Massachusetts.*

Those who viewed the exhibit were witness to the many interpretations of the show's theme "Remembering When — Rug Hookers Reminisce." Some were personal and poignant; others were wild and wacky. *Courtesy of the Wenham Museum, Wenham, Massachusetts.*

Those who came to view the exhibit were treated to hooked rugs of all sizes, shapes, and subject matters. *Courtesy of the Wenham Museum, Wenham, Massachusetts.*

Recalling a time when folks were worried about the well being of this country, newly elected President Herbert Hoover promised "A Chicken In Every Pot." Mary Sheppard Burton. 1996. 44" x 66". *Courtesy of Mary Sheppard Burton and the Wenham Museum, Wenham, Massachusetts.*

This "Lady Liberty" welcomed visitors from all over the United States, Canada, Asia, and beyond. Pat Merikallio. 1998. 36" x 24". *Courtesy of Pat Merikallio.*

"English Garden Sampler." Wendy Ullmann. 1998. 47" x 43". *Courtesy of the Wenham Museum, Wenham, Massachusetts.*

Grand not only describes the king of beasts but also the late artist that hooked their likeness. Joan Moshimer. 1997. 48" x 68". *Courtesy of the Moshimer Family and W. Cushing and Company, Kennebunkport, Maine.*

The 19th century period bedroom of the museum's Clafin-Richards House was decked out in floral splendor and filled to capacity with hooked rugs dating from the 1850s . Rugs from the private collection of James A. Turbayne and Jessie A. Turbayne. *Courtesy of the Wenham Museum, Wenham, Massachusetts*

Early rug patterns were often printed with the fashionable colors of the time. A vintage hooking frame displays a work in progress. Rugs from the private collection of James A. Turbayne and Jessie A. Turbayne. *Courtesy of the Wenham Museum, Wenham, Massachusetts.*

Three centuries meet. An array of geometric design hooked rugs from the late 19th and early 20th century add a touch of color to the museum's 18th century period room. Rugs from the private collection of James A. Turbayne and Jessie A. Turbayne. *Courtesy of the Wenham Museum, Wenham, Massachusetts.*

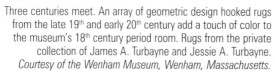

Simplicity at its best. A hooked rug of divided block pattern hangs above the hearth. Resting on the chair table is a Grenfell mat made in Labrador and fashioned after a traditional quilt pattern. Both are early 20th century. Rug and mat from the private collection of James A. Turbayne and Jessie A. Turbayne. *Courtesy of the Wenham Museum, Wenham, Massachusetts.*

Wellspring: A Folk Artist and Her Community

During the summer of 1998 the Hallockville Museum Farm and Folklife Center of Riverhead, New York, featured an exhibit by painter turned hooking artist, Gail Horton. A lifelong resident of the nearby Long Island waterfront village of Greenport, Gail began the journey of exploring her childhood through the medium of rug hooking. As she hooked her memories, what emerged was a deep appreciation for family and community; her continuous source of love and inspiration, her own personal wellspring.

"Silver Lake Hoop Snake" recalls the local legend of an infamous reptile that inhabits a secluded spot in New York's Greenport village. When any youngster nears the lake, the sinister snake puts its tail in its mouth, forming a circle, then rolls madly after the unwanted trespasser. Gail F. Horton. 1996. 31" x 31". Collection of David and Eileen Kapell. *Courtesy of Gail F. Horton.*

That which is dear to the artist is portrayed in "The Family Rug." Gail F. Horton. 1989. 24" x 36". Collection of Daniel Horton. *Courtesy of Gail F. Horton.*

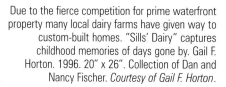

"Family Traditions" warrant that Greenport's annual Fourth of July fireworks display be viewed from either the shore or from the decks of the community's own North Ferry. Gail F. Horton. 1998. 21" x 24". Collection of Dan and Nancy Fischer. *Courtesy of Gail F. Horton.*

Due to the fierce competition for prime waterfront property many local dairy farms have given way to custom-built homes. "Sills' Dairy" captures childhood memories of days gone by. Gail F. Horton. 1996. 20" x 26". Collection of Dan and Nancy Fischer. *Courtesy of Gail F. Horton.*

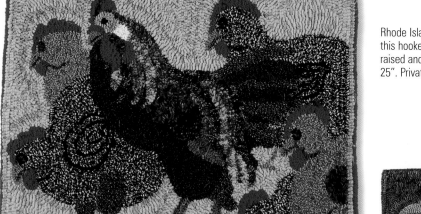

Rhode Island Reds and Plymouth Rocks strut their stuff in this hooked tribute to the feathered friends that the artist raised and loved. "The Flock." Gail F. Horton. 1998. 22" x 25". Private Collection. *Courtesy of Gail F. Horton.*

The stylized tree of life separating Sharkbait and Barney symbolizes the earth and all the creatures on it. "Pets." Gail F. Horton. 1998. 26" x 32". Collection of Julia and Harold Pleitez. *Courtesy of Gail F. Horton.*

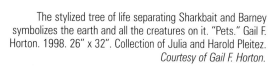

In the artist's own words, "I chose to hook the easterly view of the lighthouse with very few details as I felt this uncluttered view expresses the comforting sense of aloneness endemic to the site." "Horton's Point Lighthouse." Gail F. Horton. 1998. 24" x 24". *Courtesy of Gina Rusch.*

"Gardens" were an integral part of community life during the 1940s and 1950s. The artist and her brother are pictured picking Japanese beetles off of their neighbor's prized raspberry plants. Mrs. Terry paid the youngsters one penny for every five beetles that were captured and drowned in a jar of kerosene. Gail F. Horton. 1998. 24" x 36". Private Collection. *Courtesy of Gail F. Horton.*

Gail often visited a wondrous room in Mrs. Terry's house that was filled with yards of cloth and the worn, torn, and outgrown clothing of men, women, and children; all waiting to be recycled. "The Rag Room." Gail F. Horton. 1998. 20" x 30". Private Collection. *Courtesy of Gail F. Horton.*

During a 1986 trip to the Emerald Isle Gail discovered the many similarities between the Irish countryside and the Long Island community of her childhood. A magnificent 9th century tall cross presiding over a churchyard in Moone was the inspiration for "Three Children in the Fiery Furnace – Moone." Gail F. Horton. 1997. 22" x 22". *Courtesy of John and Aurelie Stack.*

A chance encounter with an unusual natural phenomenon remains a cherished childhood memory. "Aurora Borealis." 1998. 21" x 26.5". Collection of Joe and Nancy Townsend. *Courtesy of Gail F. Horton.*

Ducks, chickens, eggs, and farm fresh produce were available at "The Big Duck," a favorite roadside attraction. Gail F. Horton. 1986. 33" x 26". Collection of Antonia and Whitney Booth. *Courtesy of Gail F. Horton.*

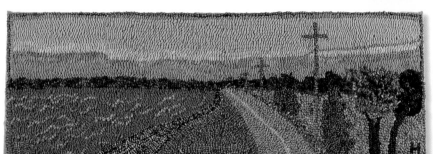

"The Road Out East" was the most beautiful of all roads. Gail F. Horton. 1997. 17" x 44". Collection of Dan and Nancy Fischer. *Courtesy of Gail F. Horton.*

"The Walter Royal," one of the many work boats instrumental in building bay channels, steams ahead on smooth seas. Gail F. Horton. 1986. 20" x 25.5". Collection of Joshua Y. Horton. *Courtesy of Gail F. Horton.*

"Sterling Creek" captures all that is the waterfront community of Greenport, New York. Gail F. Horton. 1998. 23" x 28". Collection of Rich and Marilyn Fiedler. *Courtesy of Gail F. Horton.*

The artist at work. *Courtesy of Gail F. Horton.*

Gail's hooked art has been exhibited in Ireland and throughout the United States with numerous group and solo shows in the New York area. Her work has also been featured at and sold by the South Street Seaport Museum in Lower Manhattan. She maintains a long-term relationship with the Fiedler Gallery of Greenport, New York. Gail shares her joy of hooking by teaching others the craft and lecturing on design.

Created on a monk's cloth foundation using strips of woolen fabric, Gail's work at times incorporates silk fabric and woolen yarns for added color, effect, and texture.

Her lifelong Long Island home and her interest in and on going research of ancient Irish history continues to inspire the rugs that Gail creates.

Walt Whitman's poem about Long Island was the motivating force behind "Sea Beauty – Stretched and Basking." The body and tail of a sleeping mermaid are magically transformed into the map of Long Island. Gail F. Horton. 2002. 16" x 68". *Courtesy of Gail F. Horton.*

What could be more enjoyable then gazing out across the sand and sea while relaxing in your mermaid "Beach Chair?" Gail F. Horton. 1996. 42" x 16". Collection of David Berson. *Courtesy of Gail F. Horton.*

"Eva And Nick's Wedding Rug." This sea-inspired design not only served as a requested "merperson" wedding invitation but the happy couple stood on the hooked version while taking their vows. Gail F. Horton. 2002. 31" x 41.5". From the Collection of Eva and Nick Bogaty. *Courtesy of Gail F. Horton*.

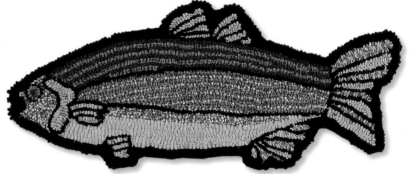

Fresh catch of the day. "Striped Bass." Gail F. Horton. 1999. 9" x 29". Collection of Peggy and Jim Murphy. *Courtesy of Gail F. Horton*.

Using Irish woolen fabrics, "Three Crosses of County Kildare" was hooked after fourteen years of research and two trips to Ireland. This tribute to Celtic history has been exhibited in Ireland and numerous sites in the United States. Gail F. Horton. 2000. 81" x 81". *Courtesy of Gail F. Horton*.

Sauder Village, Archbold, Ohio

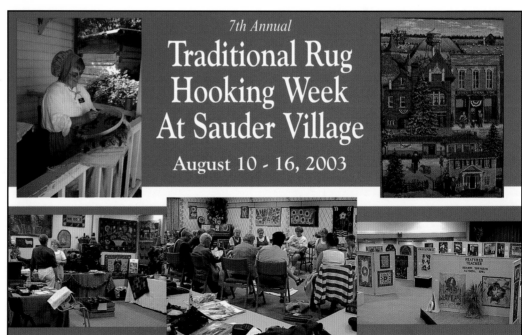

Rug hookers' paradise can be found in Archbold, Ohio. *Courtesy of Sauder Village*.

Since the 1997 conception of its annual August rug hooking workshops and exhibition, historic Sauder Village, in Archbold, Ohio, has welcomed thousands of hooking enthusiasts from across the United States and Canada. Each year hundreds of hooked works, of both original and preprinted design, are hung in Founder's Hall delighting the many visitors who anxiously await the highly anticipated event. The show is open to all rug hookers. Ribbons are awarded in a variety of categories. Some of the artists' work is offered for sale.

Hundreds of hand-hooked rugs are displayed in Founder's Hall at Sauder Village. *Courtesy of Sauder Village.*

Each year the hooked work of a featured teacher takes center stage. *Courtesy of Sauder Village.*

2002 Best of Show. "Village of Pemberville." Cindi Gay. Pemberville, Ohio. *Courtesy of Cindi Gay and Sauder Village.*

89

2001 Best of Show. "248 Overlook Drive." Sandra Brown. Pittsburgh, Pennsylvania. *Courtesy of Sauder Village.*

2001 Sauder Award. "The Freedom Quilt." Pris Butler. Gainesville, Georgia. *Courtesy of Sauder Village.*

2000 Best of Show. "Sultat." A Pearl McGown pattern. June Mikoryak. Allen Park, Michigan. *Courtesy of June Mikoryak and Sauder Village.*

2000 Sauder Award. "Summer Symphony." Dee Doria. Plymouth, Michigan. *Courtesy of Sauder Village.*

1999 Best of Show. "May The Road Rise Up To Greet You." Sandra Brown. Pittsburgh, Pennsylvania. *Courtesy of Sauder Village.*

1999 Sauder Award. "Wisconsin Farm." Emily Robertson. Milwaukee, Wisconsin. *Courtesy of Sauder Village.*

Hooked rugs of every subject matter, shape, and size delight and inspire all. *Courtesy of Sauder Village.*

The United States Embassy, Ankara, Turkey

Selected as part of the Arts in the Embassy Program of the State Department, "Café; Reading The Newspaper" by artist Roslyn Logsdon was selected to be exhibited at the United States Embassy in Ankara, Turkey, for two years, 2002 through 2004. The hooked scene was inspired by fond memories of leisure moments spent in the cafés of great cities throughout Europe. An extensive portfolio of Roslyn's work is available at her studio in the Montpelier Cultural Arts Center in Laurel, Maryland. She is also a popular rug hooking instructor.

Inspired by fond memories of leisure moments spent in the cafés of European cities, "Café: Reading The Newspaper" is currently on display at the United States Embassy in Ankara, Turkey. 1997. 20" x 21". *Courtesy of Roslyn Logsdon.*

SHOWS

The demand for textile art has made hooked rugs a popular item at many fine art shows and quality craft shows. This venue offers the hooking artist an opportunity to display their talents to an admiring and buying public.

"Brooklyn Bridge" was created for a show at the South Street Seaport Museum in New York City. Gail F. Horton. 1998. 17" x 32". *Courtesy of Rita Vanius*.

Liz Alpert Fay, Sandy Hook, Connecticut

Most definitely "High in Saturated Color." Liz Alpert Fay. 2002. 38" x 48". *Courtesy of Liz Alpert Fay*

I enjoy selling my work at craft shows where I can talk directly to people about my work and get feed back first hand. I had been pricing my work by the square foot because that is the way I saw other people arriving at prices for rugs. However, my work is evolving and I now feel more comfortable pricing it as art and not necessarily using a formula to arrive at the price.

My rugs are explorations in color. They also tell stories and reflect my views on life. I use my work to express my ideas and comment on issues that are important to me. I have taught young children for many years and I am always inspired by their fresh, direct approach. In many of my rugs I strive to create that same sense of spontaneity.

A whimsical angel welcomes customers into Liz Alpert Fay's show booth. *Courtesy of Liz Alpert Fay.*

"Rug for Aron." Interpretation of a child's drawing. 1998. 27" x 34". *Courtesy of Liz Alpert Fay.*

"Chelsea's Rug" is a collection of one child's kindergarten drawings. 1999. 38" x 63". *Courtesy of Liz Alpert Fay.*

Elaine Ducharme, Natick, Massachusetts

Elaine Ducharme is an accomplished artist in a variety of media including oils, pastels, watercolors, and clay. Her passion is for hooked rugs. She brings a unique approach to her rugs, combining her artistic talent and insights of her hooking technique. Several of her rugs are hooked adaptations of her artwork.

Elaine exhibits and sells at fine art shows throughout the New England area.

"Bella in Her Bath." Painted floor mat. Elaine Ducharme. 2000. 24" x 36". *Courtesy of Elaine Ducharme.*

"Sophia and Her Friends," the painting. Elaine Ducharme. 2001. *Courtesy of Elaine Ducharme.*

A work in progress. The hooked version of "Sophia and Her Friends," a rug that will delight one and all. 2003. 48" x 66". *Courtesy of Elaine Ducharme.*

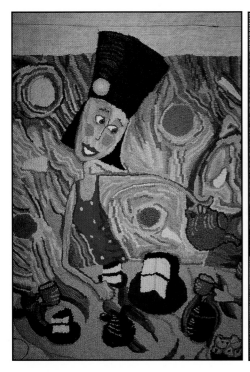

A closer look shows our hooked hostess not only pouring a spot of tea but serving a cake that even Betty Crocker would be proud of. *Courtesy of Elaine Ducharme.*

Detail of one of the girls, poised and polished. *Courtesy of Elaine Ducharme.*

Detail of another friend sporting a black beret and enthralled with the lively conversation. *Courtesy of Elaine Ducharme.*

In addition to selling completed pieces, some hookers will create rugs to your specification. The charge for commissioned work is generally a per square foot fee. Prices can range anywhere from $100 per square foot and up. The finer the strip of material hooked and more complex the design the higher the price. Expect to pay more for custom work undertaken by a noted hooking artist.

Some prefer not to charge by the square foot but will quote you a set price for the entire job. Make sure you know in advance what the finished rug will cost.

Charging by the hour can cause problems for both the artist and the consumer. Few non-hookers realize how long it actually takes to hook a rug.

Once you and the rug hooker have come to an agreement make sure you have everything in writing. Your invoice or receipt should include a description of the work, dimensions, cost, and approximate time of completion. A deposit is often required.

Mill River Rugs, Leeds, Massachusetts

The artist's business card. *Courtesy of Margaret Arraj MacDonald.*

Drawing upon her spiritual background, hooking artist Margaret Arraj MacDonald creates timeless works of art using woolen rug yarns. With each subtle detail that she hooks into a linen foundation there is a story to be told. Available through her studio, Mill River Rugs in Leeds, Massachusetts, prices for her completed pieces start at $800. She is also willing to do commissioned pieces.

In Margaret's hands woolen rug yarns are transformed into hooked works of art. *Courtesy of Margaret Arraj MacDonald.*

The intricacies of William Morris's 1879 design were deftly interpreted with hook and woolen yarns. "Dove and Rose Rug." Margaret Arraj MacDonald. 2002 . 44" x 31". *Courtesy of Margaret Arraj MacDonald.*

Amid the tragic events of September 11, 2001 and those of the war in Afghanistan, Margaret's spiritual nature compelled her to seek beauty in the art of Islam. "Islamic Tiles" was adapted from floral design ceramic tiles found in Iran's 17th century Shah Mosque. Margaret Arraj MacDonald. 2001. 33" x 48". *Courtesy of Margaret Arraj MacDonald.*

Left: While reading *Old Path, White Clouds, Walking in the Footsteps of Buddha* by Thich Nhat Hanh, Margaret was taken with the book's charming illustrations. With permission from the Vietnamese illustrators, Nguyen Thi Hop and Nguyen Dong, she combined and adapted elements of their work into her own. "Buddhist Rug." 2002. 45" x 31". *Courtesy of Margaret Arraj MacDonald.*

Right: Inspiration can be found in the most unlikely places. The ornate motif of "Silverscape Rug" was found on a bronze door panel in a building that originally housed the First National Bank. Built in 1928, the Northampton, Massachusetts property is now owned by Silverscape Designs, a jewelry company. Margaret Arraj MacDonald. 2002. 62" x 32". *Courtesy of Margaret Arraj MacDonald.*

Small and simple, "Peace Pagoda Lotus" was fashioned after a floor tile found at the Peace Pagoda in Leverett, Massachusetts. Margaret Arraj MacDonald. 2001. 18" x 18". *Courtesy of Margaret Arraj MacDonald.*

The bronze door panel that inspired "Silverscape Rug." *Courtesy of Margaret Arraj MacDonald.*

Peace Pagoda floor tile. *Courtesy of Margaret Arraj MacDonald.*

Christine Parker, Rockford, Michigan

In her spare time veterinarian, Dr. Christine Parker hooks rugs for fun and profit. Over the past ten years she has taken numerous courses in color, design, and drawing in addition to attending yearly rug hooking camps and workshops. As a member of a local art gallery and co-op her hooked rugs are proudly hung beside watercolor and oil paintings. Her ultimate goal is to have hooked rugs widely recognized as fiber art.

Most of the rugs I hook are exercises or experiments either in design or color use. It's the process as much as the product that interests me. I'm not emotional about my art and don't form attachments to the pieces. I live in a small house where I couldn't possibly use the number of rugs I've hooked so I sell them.

Opposite page, **top left:** Adapted from a quilt pattern, "Celtic Charm" would complement any décor, antique or contemporary. Christine Parker. 2000. 30" x 19". *Courtesy of Christine Parker.*

Although modern looking in design, "Contained Crazy" was actually adapted from a century's old style of quilting. Christine Parker. 2000. 33" x 33". *Courtesy of Christine Parker.*

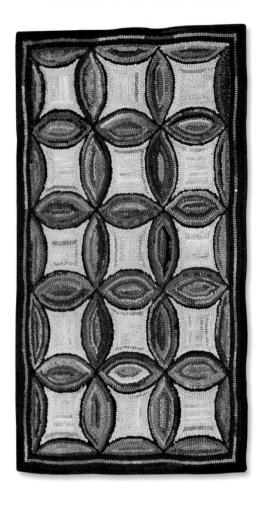

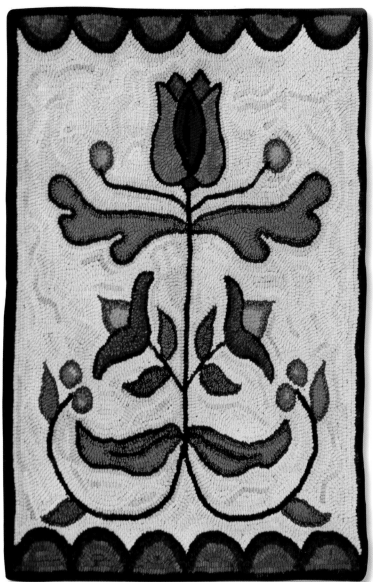

Tribute is paid to the tulip that help to destroy Holland's economy in the early 1600s. "Semper Augustus" was adapted from a popular Pennsylvania Dutch design. Christine Parker. 2001. 25" x 20". *Courtesy of Christine Parker.*

"Can't Have too Many Dishes" is the mantra of every successful host and hostess. "Dishes." Christine Parker. 1999. 30" x 38". *Courtesy of Christine Parker.*

Christine offers custom color and design work but will hook preprinted patterns as well. She also sells completed rugs of her own design. Using either a linen or monk's cloth foundation many are hooked exclusively with hand- dyed woolen fabrics. Prices for the rugs pictured start in the $300 range and go up.

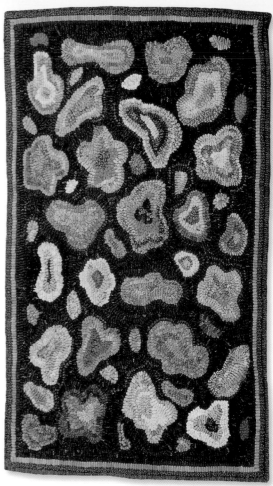

Recalling traditional quilt motifs, "Sweet Sue" is simply charming. Christine Parker. 2001. 20" x 31". *Courtesy of Christine Parker.*

"Fallen Leaves" is an abstract version of the popular cat's paw pattern. Christine Parker. 1999. 25" x 17". *Courtesy of Christine Parker.*

A Cottage Industry, McAdoo Rugs

What could be more fun than a rug full of monkeys? "Blue Monkeys." 48" x 72". *Courtesy of McAdoo Rugs, North Bennington, Vermont.*

In an age of super-sized stores and impersonal on-line buying it is comforting to know that family owned businesses offering personal service and a quality hand-made product still exist. McAdoo Rugs is such a company. Founded by Francis and Cynthia McAdoo in 1972, McAdoo Rugs was originally started as a non-profit project to bring employment to the rural people of Maine. In 1980 their son Preston took over the business and moved it to Vermont. Today he and his wife Cynthia oversee all the day-to-day operations needed to produce the quality of hand-hooked rugs that attract customers such as Kirstie Alley, Candice Bergen, George and Barbara Bush, Bill and Hilary Clinton, Glenn Close, Michael J. Fox, King Hussein, Kiri Te Kanawa, Ethel Kennedy, Norman Lear, Dudley Moore, Mary Tyler Moore, Paul Newman and Joanne Woodward, Sister Parish and Albert Hadley, Tom Selick, Meryl Streep, and Gene Wilder.

Custom-made for a lover of "Waterbirds." 7' diameter. *Courtesy of McAdoo Rugs, North Bennington, Vermont.*

A mirror image of flower and foliage takes on a tropical twist. "Birds In Paradise." 48" x 72". *Courtesy of McAdoo Rugs, North Bennington, Vermont.*

Seaweed frames a multitude of "Striped Bass." 48" x 72". *Courtesy of McAdoo Rugs, North Bennington, Vermont.*

Ancient denizens of the deep join winged waterfowl. "Medieval Sea Creatures." 36" x 55". *Courtesy of McAdoo Rugs, North Bennington, Vermont.*

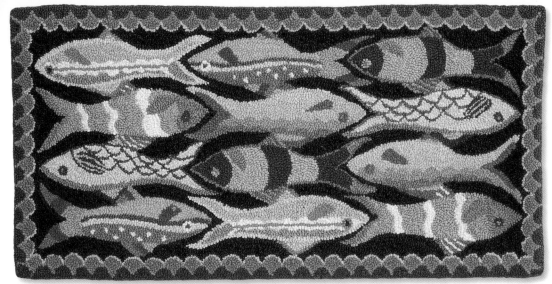

Lined up and ready to attend "Fish School." 23" x 48".
Courtesy of McAdoo Rugs, North Bennington, Vermont.

In the words of Preston and Cynthia McAdoo:

We are a cottage industry in North Bennington, Vermont. McAdoo rugs are individually hooked by hand in the homes of those we employee. They are made of 100% virgin New Zealand and English rug wool that is spun in Philadelphia and hand-dyed by us in North Bennington. We use the most colorfast dyes available. Fading in the sun is minimal. All rugs are hooked on a heavy cotton monk's cloth foundation. The dense weave holds the loops so tightly in place that applying latex on the back is not necessary. Without a backing dirt does not become trapped and rugs can be easily cleaned, dried, and repaired if necessary. Research shows that latex may also be toxic while it is being applied and after it has dried. Our rugs will last a lifetime and we will happily repair any mishaps caused by teething puppies.

McAdoo hooked rugs are made with pride in America. Each rug is personally inspected and is often changed even after it is completed. Moving our manufacturing overseas would demand an increase in production that would severely jeopardize design quality. In addition to our show room inventory of original copyrighted designs we welcome custom orders starting at around $100 per square foot plus a custom design fee. Often before any work is started customers receive full size drawings of their rug complete with color samples. This way we can be sure you are getting exactly what you hoped for.

Custom-made for a "Trout" fan. 43" x 64". *Courtesy of McAdoo Rugs, North Bennington, Vermont.*

Our North Bennington mill houses our rug showroom and provides studio space for designing and dyeing. McAdoo hooked rugs are also available in various stores throughout the United States.

"Bulldog," a hooked portrait of a favorite pet. 24" x 31". *Courtesy of McAdoo Rugs, North Bennington, Vermont.*

Custom-made "Begging Bassets" captures four furry friends at rest. 24" x 30". *Courtesy of McAdoo Rugs, North Bennington, Vermont.*

A whimsical "Leopard" to delight all ages. 25" x 40". *Courtesy of McAdoo Rugs, North Bennington, Vermont.*

Customers can choose from over 300 designs or have a hooked rug custom-made.

A chase takes place along the perimeters of "Stag Hunt." 50" x 72". *Courtesy of McAdoo Rugs, North Bennington, Vermont.*

A rich-toned runner with a limited and pleasing palette. "Cheetah." 32" x 111". *Courtesy of McAdoo Rugs, North Bennington, Vermont.*

Tribute is paid to the Father of our Country. "George Washington On A Horse." 30" x 36". *Courtesy of McAdoo Rugs, North Bennington, Vermont.*

Reminiscent of traditional hooked rug designs, "Antique Oak Leaf" was custom-made for a client with discriminating taste. 106" x 90". *Courtesy of McAdoo Rugs, North Bennington, Vermont.*

McAdoo Rugs are hooked from woolen yarns using an Oxford Punch Needle, a close cousin to the traditional rug hook.

CATALOGS AND DEPARTMENT STORES

Many mail order catalogs and department stores offer hooked rugs for sale. Do be aware that typically these are mass-produced by machine with a limited amount of actual handwork. Machine-made hooked rugs will not increase in value over time. They are decorative floor coverings and should be used and enjoyed as such.

Pictured is a mass-produced machine-made hooked rug that was available in scatter, area, and room-size.1960-1980. 24" x 36".

The overall uniform look of a machine-made hooked rug is evident in this close-up. Cotton rug yarn, with no variation in tone, width, or texture, is used throughout the entire rug. The hooking style is very precise and mechanical and lacks the subtle qualities of true handwork.

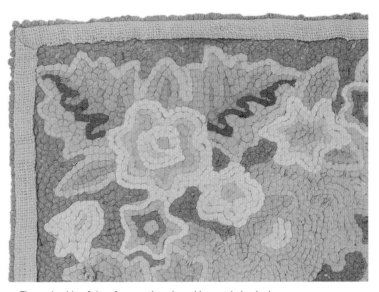

The underside of the aforementioned machine-made hooked rug.

Chapter Seven

Hooking Your Own

Her majesty, "The Almost Virgin Queen," poses with royal hook in hand. A self-portrait. Pat Merikallio. 2002. 46" x 36". *Courtesy of Pat Merikallio.*

Don't forget the option of hooking your own rug. The craft is easy to master, nourishes your creative side, and reduces stress. There are qualified instructors available as well as how-to- books. Suppliers offer everything needed to hook a rug from start to finish. If designing a rug is not for you there are thousands of pre-printed patterns to choose from.

As previously mentioned many rug makers hook just for pleasure with no intentions of selling. Their work is meant to delight family, friends, fellow rug hookers, and readers of this book.

The roaring surf serves as a backdrop for a wide-eyed "Ben." Pat Merikallio. 2000. 44" x 52". *Courtesy of Pat Merikallio.*

Framed with lush flowers and foliage, "The Guardian" protects two tiny tots. Pat Merikallio. 1998. 41" x 48". *Courtesy of Pat Merikallio.*

"Boris," a dog of Oriental ancestry, holds court on a carpet of similar heritage. Pat Merikallio. 1989. 31" x 41". *Courtesy of Pat Merikallio.*

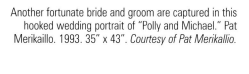

Twisting and turning, "Sea Otters" play in calm waters. Pat Merikallio. 2001. 25" x 36". *Courtesy of Pat Merikallio..*

Hooked to honor the celebration of "Kirsti and Matt's Wedding" and this country's Independence Day. Pat Merikallio. 1994. 47" x 55". *Courtesy of Pat Merikallio.*

Another fortunate bride and groom are captured in this hooked wedding portrait of "Polly and Michael." Pat Merikaillo. 1993. 35" x 43". *Courtesy of Pat Merikaillo.*

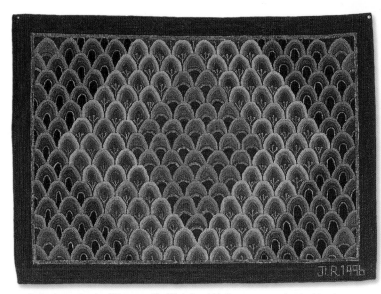

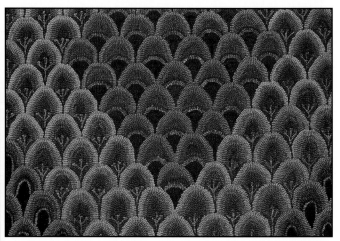

Close-up of "Vermont Shell." *Courtesy of June Robbs.*

A timeless classic. "Vermont Shell." A Pearl McGown pattern hooked by June Robbs. 1996. 28" x 40". *Courtesy of June Robbs.*

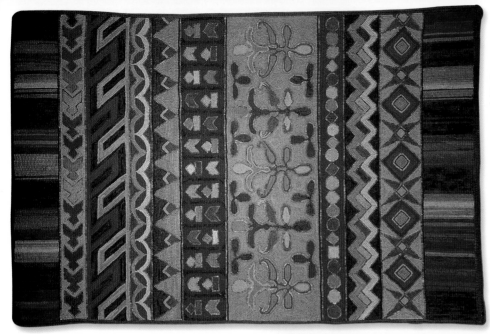

"Veda" was inspired by a rug from Henry Ford's Dearborn, Michigan boyhood home. June Robbs. 1999. 38" x 58". *Courtesy of June Robbs.*

Many hooked rug patterns imitate quilt patterns. "Illusion." Pearl McGown pattern. Hooked by June Robbs. 2000. 28" x 46". *Courtesy of June Robbs.*

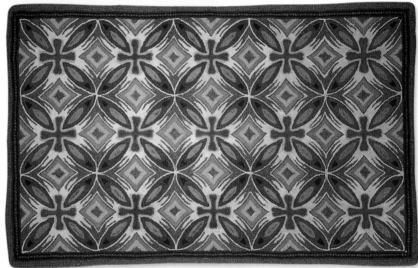

Adapted from a late 19th century German postcard, "Goodnight Irene Goodnight" warns to "Watch your step tis Halloween. Time when witches & spooks convene." June Robbs. 2002. 28" x 41". *Courtesy of June Robbs.*

All rug makers dream of wool not yet hooked. "Wool Dreaming." Diane Phillips. 1998. 26" x 36". *Courtesy of Diane Phillips.*

"Madame Zola," star of the circus, entertains all. Diane Phillips. 1998. 27" x 33". *Courtesy of Diane Phillips.*

"Give Me Liberty, Give Me Wool" is the creed of every rug hooker with attitude. Diane Phillips. 2001. 29" x 28". *Courtesy of Diane Phillips.*

In a style reminiscent of Outsider Art, a determined "Leader Of The Pack" rushes to reach her goal with Olive, the Chihuahua, in tow. Diane Phillips. 2002. 30" x 48". *Courtesy of Diane Phillips.*

Even from her heavenly domain the strength of a beloved "Grandmother" can be felt. Diane Phillips. 2002. 29" x 36". *Courtesy of Diane Phillips.*

Bits of reality are to be found among the abstract. "Atlantis." Susan Smidt. 2002. 40" x 25". *Courtesy of Susan Smidt.*

A tribute to a William Morris tapestry. "Sir William." Canadian hooking artist Sybil Mercer. 1993. 32" x 26". *Courtesy of Sybil Mercer.*

Hooked to the delight of her "School Bus" loving grandson, Jake. Susan Smidt. 1997. 31" x 28". *Courtesy of Susan Smidt.*

"The Fox," companion to "Sir William." Both were horizontally hooked to replicate the original tapestry. Sybil Mercer. 1995. 32" x 26". *Courtesy of Sybil Mercer*.

"My Mother's Garden" actually depicts the artist's lupine garden but was named for the woman whose coat was used to hook the greenery. The colorful blooms were prodded, one of the oldest forms of hooking. Sybil Mercer. 1999. 24" x 16". *Courtesy of Sybil Mercer.*

A Victorian walnut screen holds "Garden of Seasons." The hooked panels, each 53" x 22", highlight the glory of Sybil's garden during spring, summer, and fall. Lake Huron and the continually changing sky set the backdrop. Recipient of the Ontario Hooking Craft Guild 2000 Best of Show. Sybil Mercer. 1999. *Courtesy of Sybil Mercer*.

A close-up of "Garden of Seasons." *Courtesy of Sybil Mercer*.

"Afternoon Delight," a self-portrait designed by Michele Micarelli and her brother Ralph Caparulo, has delighted many including the rug hooker it portrays. Woolen fabric on linen with yarn and metallic fabric embellishments. Michele Micarelli. 2002. 29" x 32". *Courtesy of Michele Micarelli.*

This hooked symbol of hospitality would be welcomed in any home. "Pineapple Antique." Quail Hill Design. Hooked by June Mikoryak. 1985. 36.5" x 72". *Courtesy of June Mikoryak.*

"Iris Panel." A floral still life created from strips of woolen fabric. Jane Flynn pattern. June Mikoryak. 1998. 24" x 12". *Courtesy of June Mikoryak.*

Inspired by an antique hooked rug of simple "Hit or Miss Stripe" design. June Mikoryak. 2001. 37" x 72". *Courtesy of June Mikoryak.*

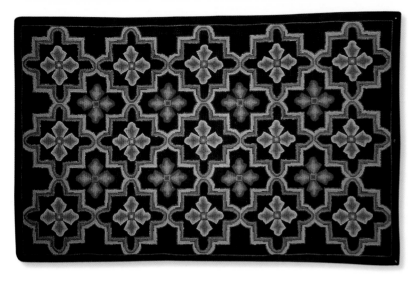

"Fletcher Geometric" is an intricate motif handled in a lively manner. Pearl McGown pattern. June Mikoryak. 1998. 35.5" x 56". *Courtesy of June Mikoryak.*

A self-portrait, "Kiss The Bird" uses the image of a crow to symbolize loss of people and places once held dear. The bird speaks to this loss but also inspires ideas of renewal and replacement. Jo-Ann Millen. 2001. 30" x 27". *Courtesy of Jo-Ann Millen.*

"Judea," a Patsy Becker design, was hooked and enhanced by Mary Jane Patchell. 2002. 20" x 30". *Courtesy of Mary Jane Patchell.*

"Footprints." Recalling days spent on the shore of Lake Huron as the sun sets behind Chantry Island, a protected bird sanctuary. This childhood scene by Canadian hooking artist Barbara Nonnewitz received the Ontario Hooking Craft Guild 2002 Pictorial Award. 1999. 24" x 30". *Courtesy of Barbara Nonnewitz.*

"Swimming In The Leaves" was inspired by a photograph of her two sons at play. In addition to traditional hooking, the age-old technique of prodding was used to create the fall foliage. Barbara Nonnewitz. 2000. 33" x 42". *Courtesy of Barbara Nonnewitz.*

If designing your own rug is not an option, suppliers offer a wide variety of preprinted patterns. Pictured is a portion of "Full Basket," hooking scissors, and selection of hand-dyed woolen fabrics from New Earth Designs. *Courtesy of Jeanne Benjamin / New Earth Designs.*

"Christmas In The Country," a nighttime village scene framed in a traditional quilt pattern, was designed and hooked by Jeanne Benjamin using the woolen fabrics that she hand-dyes. 1998. 31.5" x 42". *Courtesy of Jeanne Benjamin / New Earth Designs.*

How does your hooked rug grow? One strip of woolen fabric at a time. A work in progress that would make Georgia O'Keeffe smile. Designed and hooked by Judy Yasi. 2002. One in a series of floral blocks each 11" x 11". *Courtesy of Judy Yasi.*

A sampler of shapes and designs. "Century Antique" is a fun and easy pattern to hook. Designed and hooked by Jeanne Benjamin. 2002. 19" x 36". *Courtesy of Jeanne Benjamin / New Earth Designs.*

A close-up of "Century Antique." *Courtesy of Jeanne Benjamin / New Earth Designs.*

Life can be full of confrontations. "Standoff: Samson v. Kitty Mom." Cindi Gay. 2001. 31" x 53". *Courtesy of Cindi Gay.*

Based on Maine coast images, real and fanciful, "The Realm Of The Unicorn" was a group project that brought together those experienced in natural dyeing, spinning, and rug hooking. The hooked tapestry, six years in the making, is permanently on display at the Humboldt Field Research Institute in Steuben, Maine. Designed by Rose Wirtz. Hooked by Cecilia Clement, Linda Rae Coughlin, Nancy Hillenburg, Joerg-Henner Lotze, and Rose Wirtz. 1996-2002. 46.5" x 60". *Courtesy of Rose Wirtz.*

Detail of "Realm Of The Unicorn." *Courtesy of Rose Wirtz.*

121

Chapter Eight

Condition

When starting a collection of anything it is always prudent to seek out the best that you can find and afford. This is a very good rule to follow but of course there are exceptions to every rule, particularly when it comes to collecting hand-hooked rugs.

This primitive and pleasing still life of flowers in a compote basket is in excellent condition, mounted, and ready to hang. Of New England or New York origins. 1890-1910. 20" x 34". *Private Collection.*

A sizable Grenfell hooked mat with strong color and in excellent condition. Grenfell Labrador Industries. Early 20th century. 15" x 49". *Private Collection.*

Originally intended for floor use and subjected to daily foot traffic, few old hooked rugs have survived in pristine condition. Due to the public's growing interest, limited supply, and rising prices, antique and collectible hooked rugs are sought after regardless of condition. Some dealers will only offer hooked rugs that have been cleaned and restored. Others will sell them as is. Condition is an important factor when pricing and buying any hooked rug. As the amount of damage goes up the price should go down.

This generation of contemporary hand-hooked rugs receive far more respect than their ancestors did. They suffer less and survive longer. When purchasing new hand-hooked rugs expect them to be in good condition.

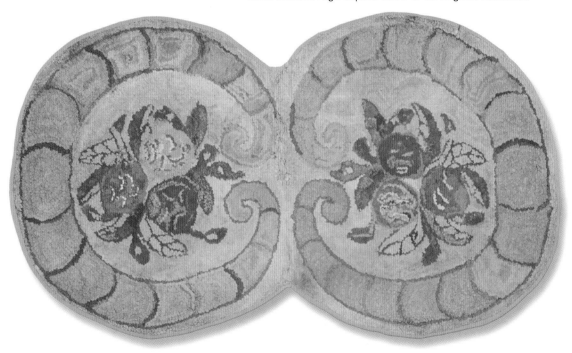

Of unusual configuration and most likely cut down from a larger rug. Horn-like C-shaped scrolls surround twin bouquets. Older make-do repairs can often add rustic charm to a hooked rug. Of New England origins. 1870-1890. *Collection of Sidney and Elizabeth Stewart.*

It is rare to find hooked rugs with age that have never been used. Hooked on a preprinted pattern using cotton fabrics and jute twine. Canadian Maritime origins. 1950-1970. 19" x 40".

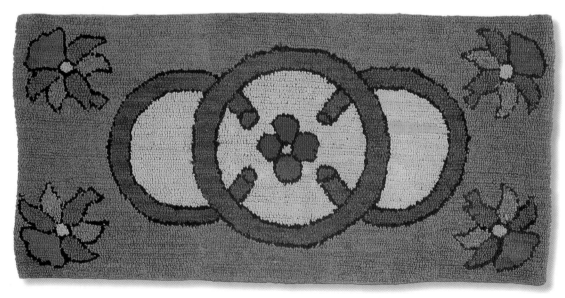

Expect to find newer hand-hooked rugs in good to excellent condition. The aquatint, "Capturing A Sperm Whale," served as inspiration for the late Virginia Sheldon's hooked seascape. 1981. 35" x 52".

Any new hooked work purchased or commissioned directly from the artist should be in excellent condition when you receive it. "Friends." Roslyn Logsdon. 2001. 18.5" x 21". *Courtesy of Roslyn Logsdon*.

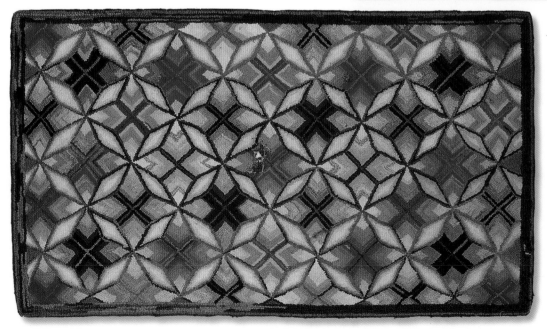

Minor damage should not deter you from adding such an exceptional rug to your collection. The small center hole was professionally repaired and the damage is no longer detectable. 1890-1910. 32" x 54". *Courtesy of Jeanne Benjamin / New Earth Designs*.

Chapter Nine

Pests and Problems:
What to Buy – What to Avoid

Man, beasts, and machines can and do inflict damage to hooked rugs. The following pages will inform you about problems that you may encounter. The intention is not to scare you away from acquiring hooked rugs but to educate you with the information needed to make wise decisions.

HOLES AND EDGE DAMAGE

Hand-hooked rugs first appeared in North American homes during the mid- to late 1800s. They decorated and warmed floors and padded generations of busy feet. After years of hard use it was not uncommon for hooked rugs to develop holes and worn edges.

A man's home is his castle even if it is a little ragged around the edges. The perimeters of a hooked rug are generally the first to show signs of wear. Loose ends can be neatly stitched back in place adding fabric when necessary. Securing the edges prevents further unraveling and will not jeopardize the rug's antique value. A few small repairs are warranted to remedy the interior damage. 1880-1900. 24" x 37".

A stag and its younger companion pause on an oasis of greenery. Made by the same hand as the aforementioned castle rug, this fine example of an early hooked rug, complete with its cotton calico hooked background, is well worth restoring. 1880-1900. 32" x 65".

The invention of the vacuum cleaner in the early 1900s was indeed a boon for housewives. As the carpet cleaning machine grew in strength and number it quickly became the leading enemy of hand-hooked rugs.

Repetitive suction of a vacuum cleaner can weaken and eventually break the foundation upon which a rug is hooked. Foundation breaks usually go unnoticed until they are large enough or numerous enough to develop into visible holes. Also vulnerable are the edges of a hand-hooked rug. Easily sucked up into the cleaner, edges often have to be manually dislodged from the machine resulting in frayed, chewed up, and torn perimeters. Vacuum cleaners equipped with additional rotating brushes inflict even greater damage. Stiff spinning bristles prematurely wear off the top surfaces of hooked loops. Such things as teething puppies and clawing cats can also be blamed for creating holes and fraying a rug's edges, but after more than 30 years of doing restoration I can state without hesitation that the majority of damage done to hand-hooked rugs is the result of overzealous vacuuming.

Nineteen eighteen would definitely benefit from a little edge repair. Dated 1918 and of the period. 25" x 76".

Simple country-style hooked rugs are always in demand. The edge of this checkerboard pattern needs to be built up and rehooked with vintage fabrics. 1910-1930. 18" x 39".

In the hands of a professional restorer this delightful rug can be returned to its former glory. Being hooked entirely from woolen yarns, the repairs should also be made with appropriate woolen yarns. 1890-1910. 31" x 54".

126

Do not shy away from acquiring a hooked rug with minor problems. Those who do repair work should be able to hand sew and rework small holes. Frayed edges can be reinforced by hand stitching, rehooking and/or binding. Numerous and gaping holes present more of a challenge to your wallet and to the person who does repair work but are not impossible to fix. Holes and torn edges should never be repaired using glue, rubber cement, latex, duck tape, heat fusing materials, or iron on patches. Doing so drastically reduces the aesthetic and monetary value of any hand-hooked rug and makes future repairs, if possible, more challenging and costly.

Cut down and rebound many years ago this floral hooked rug, initialed, dated, and displaying an original single navy blue spandrel, would be a good candidate for restoration. Rug makers used what was available and if they ran out of one color fabric another was used. Holes need to be mended and re-hooked. The binding can be undone and edges rebuilt, but often it is best to leave the old functioning binding in place. A professional restorer would be able to advise you on the proper procedure. Dated 1896 and of the period. 27" x 40".

A machine zig-zag stitch (not visible in the photo) was used to secure unraveling edges. The make-do repairs did no harm to the rug and can easily be undone. 1920-1940. 17" x 36".

Antique hooked rugs on linen are uncommon, sought after, and if in good condition demand prices starting in the thousands. Known for its durability, linen fared better over time than burlap. White areas appearing on this floral hooked rug are not holes but the still-intact linen foundation minus the hooked loops. The bald areas can be re-hooked with appropriate fabrics. 1850-1870. 23" x 47".

Starting in the 1930s and up until his death in 1987 Quebec artist and rug hooker George-Edouard Tremblay and his able students created hooked images of the local landscape. At first glance this Tremblay scene, completed with the artist's initials, appears to be in good condition. Closer examination of the puckering on the right hand side (near the most distant house) reveals that a 2" hole was stitched shut with needle and thread. The stitching can easily be undone and the hole properly fixed and rehooked with cotton yarns. 1940-1960. 30" x 37".

Another scenic Tremblay mat. The burlap foundation along the edge is intact but needs to be rehooked. Loose burlap showing along the left hand edge should be stitched to the underside of the mat forming a hem. 1940-1960. 20" x 26".

A Grenfell mat for $25? This damaged piece was purchased in a second hand shop in Massachusetts. Similar mats in good condition start in the $1000 range and go up. Restoration is possible, but, regardless of how well done the repairs are, the mat will never have the monetary value of its unblemished mate. Grenfell Labrador Industries. Early 20th century. 24" x 39".

Damaged hooked rugs are often repaired by sewing burlap patches on the underside of the rug and reworking missing areas with appropriate fabrics. This is an acceptable way to mend a hole and should not deter you from purchasing any hooked rug. Prices will reflect the number of patches and the quality of the repairs.

A rug of a dog is a "dog" of a rug most likely because of repetitive vacuuming. Restoration is possible. Found in a Quincy, Michigan farmhouse. 1870-1890. 35" x 50".

Regardless of age, no hand-hooked rug is immune to vacuum cleaner damage. A preprinted pattern. 1960-1970. 27" x 37".

Placed under the care of a professional hooked rug restorer Mr. Pug can regain his lost anatomy and go on to delight one and all for years to come. 1900-1920. 27" x 39".

Quality restoration work should go unnoticed. Poor color matching makes these background repairs stand out detracting from the rug's aesthetic appeal and monetary value. 1880-1900. 26" x 35".

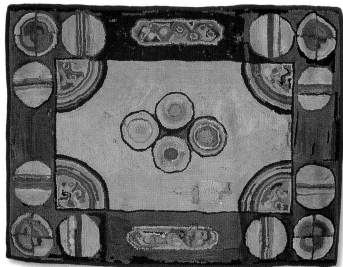

Originally hooked with an all-over solid blue border, the addition of a darker blue repair does not complement the rug and should be redone. Hooked from a preprinted pattern. 1960-1970. 20" x 32".

So what's a little hole or two or three? To discard this wonderful example of early hooked folk art would be a shame. Placed against an onion skin-dyed cotton background, primitive lollipop-like flowers spring forth from a fanciful vase. Repairs would be painstaking and time consuming but possible. 1860-1880. 24" x 34".

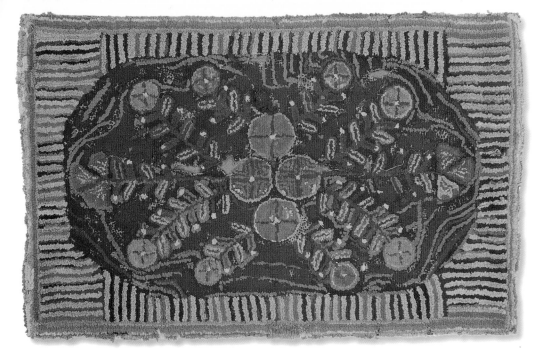

Flowers and stems shoot off like fireworks from a central four-flower medallion. Interior and edges require attention but can be repaired. 1860-1880. 26" x 42".

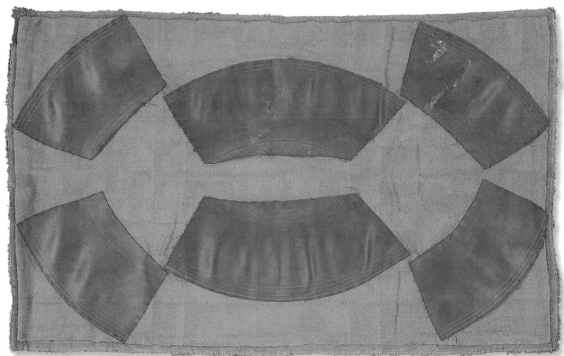

The underside of the aforementioned rug reveals that, in addition to a sewn on burlap backing, sections of rubber inner tube were stitched in place to prevent slipping when placed on the floor. Decades-old make-do remedies such as this should be preserved if at all possible. As part of the rug's history they add a note of whimsical charm.

Always visually and physically inspect any hooked rug before buying it. The edge damage is the least of this rug's problems. A thorough check reveals that there are dozens of small tears throughout the rug. E. S. Frost preprinted pattern. 1870-1890. 26" x 50".

DRY ROT AND MILDEW

Avoid buying any hooked rugs that show signs of dry rot. The price may be a bargain but the condition is not. Dry rot occurs when a hooked rug is stored for long periods of time in a very hot and dry place, such as an attic. Under these conditions the burlap foundation of the rug changes color, looses suppleness, and becomes brittle. Even minimal handling, such as bending the rug, causes the foundation threads to break, crumble, and disintegrate, leaving behind a residue of fine sawdust-like particles. Prone to frequent tears

Pictured is an unfinished 1940s hooked rug that endured over 50 summers in a hot attic. The resulting condition known as dry rot causes the burlap foundation to become very dry, discolor, and break into bits when handled. A new piece of burlap resting on top of the damaged foundation emphasizes the color change that can occur.

and holes hooked rugs with dry rot are not suitable for floor use. The foundation will continue to disintegrate. Repairs, if possible, can be frustrating, time consuming, and costly. Undertaking such a task is like trying to sew bits of sawdust together. Backing the rug with another piece of burlap or linen can add support, but will not stop the rug from deteriorating.

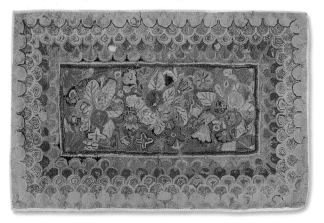

Handsome to the eye but fragile to the touch. The burlap foundation of this circa 1860 hooked rug is very brittle due to dry rot. Each time it is handled chunks of the rug break off in your hands.

A scenic hooked rug of earthy tones that is suitable only for wall hanging due to dry rot. If subjected to foot traffic it would quickly fall apart. 1880-1900. 28" x 44".

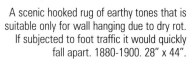

Mildew, a fungi that thrives in damp cellars of many homes, can also ruin a hooked rug. Prolonged exposure to moisture rots both the rug's foundation and the hooked loops. Often you can see the presence of mold. A musty unclean odor is detectable and certain colors of the rug may show signs of running. When handled chunks of the mildewed rug easily break off in your hand. Shy away from buying any hooked rug that has extensive mildew damage. Small damaged areas can sometimes be repaired or replaced but be prepared to pay for what is a difficult restoration job.

MOTHS

Snug as a bug in a rug is not a pleasant image for the owner of any hooked rug.

In recent years those who buy, sell, and collect vintage textiles are on alert for sightings of a silent, tiny, winged enemy. The numbers of cloth damaging moths (case-making and webbing) seem to have increased, as has their appetite for favorite fabrics. If you familiarize yourself with the telltale signs that these insects leave behind, you will know to walk away from any infested rug.

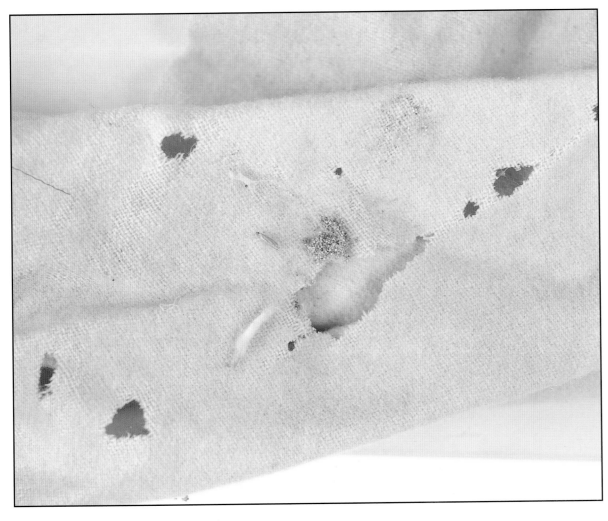

This piece of woolen fabric shows it all; moth eggs, the spun cotton-like larvae feeding tubes or cocoons, a dead moth, and the holes chewed by the feeding larvae.

Female webbing clothes moths (most commonly found in today's homes) can lay one hundred or more eggs at a time. Avoiding fresh air and sunlight, they seek out soiled fabrics (especially wool) upon which to lay their eggs. Left undisturbed the eggs develop into larvae, a worm-like feeding form that can take as little as a month or as long as four years to mature into a moth.[1] Larvae feed on woolen cloth and yarn, as well as other fabrics that have been stained with food or have been in contact with human hair or animal fur, sweat, body oils, feces or urine. They cannot survive on clean fabrics. It is the larvae not the adult flying moths that damage your hooked rugs.

The residue left by webbing clothes moths is sometimes visible. Light colored, spun cotton-like tubes less than ½ inch in length that can become affixed to a rug are the past or present dwelling of damaging larvae. Outside the feeding tube live larvae are worm-like, ½ inch long or less. They wiggle when disturbed. The bodies of dead moths and the presence of tiny sand-like particles (moth eggs) are also indicators of potential problems.

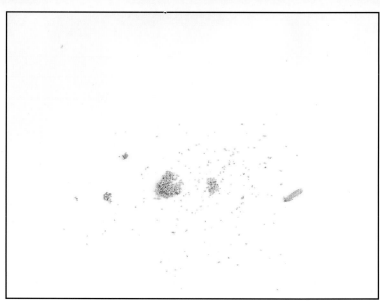

Tiny moth eggs will easily become dislodged and fall from a moth infested rug when it is handled.

Carefully examine any hooked rug that you may consider adding to your collection. Cotton-like feeding tubes are the past or present homes of damaging larvae. Their presence spells trouble.

The loops of a moth eaten hooked rug will easily crumble and fall from the foundation when prodded. Hungry larvae are not particular. They will feed on the top or underside of a dirty rug leaving behind bald areas, holes, and a brittle foundation.

Many of those who do repair work (including myself) will not accept hooked rugs that show signs of moth damage. The risk of infecting one's work place and inventory is too high. Restoration, if possible, is time consuming and expensive. Some will attempt to do repair work only after the rug has been treated with a special deep freeze process. Several days of below freezing temperatures will kill moth larvae and not harm the hooked rug. Prolonged exposures to temperatures above 100 degrees will also kill moth larvae but this method is not recommended. Extreme heat causes fabrics to dry out and become fragile. Pyrethrin, an insecticide formulated from the pyrethrum members of the chrysanthemum flower family, works by means of dehydration. Available in spray and powder form, pyrethrin based products are very effective in killing moth larvae but should be used with caution. Mothballs, flakes, and crystals will kill moths, their eggs and larvae but only when the strong vapors are contained in airtight containers. Hooked rugs should not be kept in airtight containers for an extended period of time. All textiles need to breathe.

Unfortunately when a hooked rug is actively infested and damaged beyond the point of repair the best solution to prevent widespread infestation is to dispose of the rug in a tightly sealed plastic bag. I dread this ending but I would rather lose one rug than put an entire collection at risk.

MOTH PREVENTION

The best defense against moths is cleanliness. Examine, clean, and air out your hooked rugs in the sunshine on a regular basis. Rest assured that the majority of hooked rugs that you find will be moth free. No reputable dealer would sell an infested rug. Their reputation is at stake.

Mothballs, flakes, and crystals will repel moths looking for a place to lay eggs but should never come in direct contact with your rug. For short-term storage put mothballs in a separate porous pouch (an old white sock works well) and place with your clean hooked rugs in an enclosure where vapors cannot easily escape such as a trunk or chest. When storing rugs in a closet first make sure the rugs and the closet are clean and moth free. Hang the pouch of mothballs above the hooked rugs. The strong vapors travel downward. Examine your rugs periodically and replace mothballs when needed. Naphthalene, the main ingredient in mothballs and similar products, can be dangerous to your health and should not be continuously inhaled.

Natural alternatives such as cedar wood and cedar sprays repel moths from clean fabrics but will not kill larvae. The scent from lavender, clove, camphor, and eucalyptus is also offensive to moths but will not kill the insect, its eggs or larvae.

Contemporary rug hookers when storing woolen fabrics often tuck heavily scented bars of soap or perfumed dryer sheets (used to eliminate static) in with their stash. Moths do not like strong smells.

FADING: PREMATURE AND NATURAL

The demand for antique hooked rugs is greater than the supply. Due to this demand prices are often high. In your search for hooked rugs you may come across a rug that someone has tried to prematurely age by means of chemical fading. A solution of water and household bleach lightly sponged on the top of a rug produces an even but unnatural fading. The misguided reasoning for chemically speeding up the fading process is that a faded rug is perceived as being an old rug and old rugs bring more money. Anyone with even limited knowledge of textiles will quickly realize that something is wrong. Fading from the sun occurs gradually. Under normal conditions sunlight will fade some colors and some fabrics but not all colors and all fabrics and certainly not all at the same time. Some deception artists go so far as to bleach both sides of the rug. Natural fading will only occur on the side exposed to prolonged sunlight, not both. Direct contact with household bleach can weaken and rot fabric fibers of a hooked rug and often will leave a lingering chemical smell. Fortunately these prematurely faded rugs are few and far between. The aesthetic appeal and monetary value of any chemically faded hooked rug has also dramatically faded.

Most older hooked rugs will have some colors that have naturally faded. Fading is part of the aging process and should not stop you from acquiring any older hooked rug. In some cases natural fading of certain colors actually improves the rug's aesthetics.

Faded areas can often be pulled out and rehooked but this can jeopardize the value of the rug. Consult a professional hooked rug restorer before considering this option. Sometimes it is best just to leave things alone.

The original colors used to hook this preprinted pattern of a flamingo have naturally faded to a soft pleasing palette. 1940-1950. 27.5" x 47". *Courtesy of Mark Perry and Dee DiNallo.*

Hooked in the early 1900s in Newfoundland and Labrador and sold to support the medical missionary work of Dr. Wilfred Grenfell, Grenfell mats were often fashioned from a limited selection of subtly shaded fabrics. This unusually large mat of geese flying in formation was never bright to begin with and has naturally faded over time. 38" x 62".

The underside reveals the mat's original colors in comparison to those that have faded. Hooked from finely cut strips of cotton flannel. Dyed cotton tends to fade faster than wool.

The underside of the aforementioned flamingo rug shows that some of the cotton and woolen fabrics were originally bright yellow, pink, and green. When subjected to prolonged strong sunlight cotton tends to fade faster than wool. *Courtesy of Mark Perry and Dee DiNallo.*

DOCTORING COLORS

While some deception artists are busy fading colors, others are adding colors. Prolonged exposure to strong sunlight may fade only certain areas of a hooked rug. Paint, colored markers, and dye solutions are an improper quick fix used to revitalize faded fabrics. Close examination of a recolored area reveals that the very top of the fabric or yarn loops has the strongest color. The strongest colors are naturally closest to the foundation where the fabrics are protected from sunlight and wear. Color matches in doctored rugs are often poor. Unless meticulously applied colors will bleed into surrounding areas giving the hooked rug a muddy look. Future cleaning can mean more bleeding of colors unless permanent textile markers, paints, or dyes were used. Avoid hooked rugs with artificially enhanced colors. Their monetary and aesthetic values are not as bright as their artificial coloring.

LATEX

Latex or rubber cement should never be used to patch a hole, secure frayed edges or be applied directly to a hand-hooked rug to prevent it from slipping on hardwood floors. The gooey painted-on substance adheres to the rug's foundation and hooked loops and when dried can leave your rug either stiff or rubbery depending upon the products used. This quick fix method of restoration drastically reduces the rug's monetary value as well as the possibility of future repairs. The application of latex or rubber cement should never be perceived as a means of preservation. Avoid buying antique or collectible hand-hooked rugs with total coverage or large areas of latex or rubber cement. Small latex patches are not so objectionable, but the rug's selling price should reflect their presence.

A heavy application of latex was applied to the underside of this circa 1880 hooked rug as a means of preservation. The rug is now so stiff it can literally stand up by itself. The latex backing cannot be removed, restoration is impossible, and all monetary value is gone.

A hooked rug small in size makes a bold and bright statement. After showing signs of wear and tear, a cotton twill binding was placed around its perimeters. Of Canadian origins. 1960-1970. 15" x 28".

Closer examination of the underside of the aforementioned rug shows that instead of being hand stitched latex was used to secure the binding in place. The rug's edges are very rigid making future repairs difficult.

Applying a backing of latex and burlap will drastically devalue any hand-hooked rug. This is definitely the wrong thing to do.

Iron on patches and tape and fusible fabrics all require high heat in order to bond. When heat from a household iron is applied the bonding agent on the patch or tape is activated, melts, and penetrates into hooked fabrics fusing the patch to your rug. These quick fix methods of mending should never be used to repair any hand-hooked rug. Iron on patches and tape can sometimes be removed by carefully reapplying heat from an iron. To avoid scorching the surrounding fabrics keep the iron constantly moving. When the bonding agent has softened cautiously peel away the patch using a pair of twee-

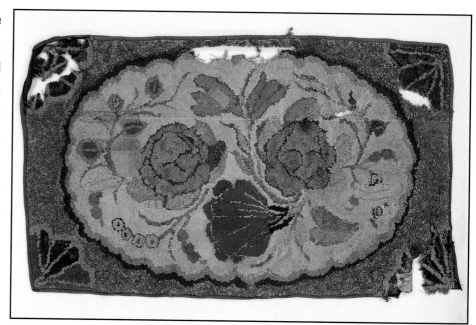

After seeing just the top side of this charming antique hooked rug one might deem it a good candidate for restoration. A more thorough examination is needed. 1880-1890. 23" x 38".

zers. Be careful not to burn your fingers. Residue from the bonding agent can remain, leaving areas of your rug stiff, scratchy to the touch, and difficult to work on if repairs are warranted. When considering a hooked rug previously repaired with iron on patches, tape, or fusible fabrics carefully check to see if a corner of the patch can be lifted. If so this is a good indicator that the ironed on areas can be removed. In some cases, if you can live with them, and no further repair is called for, it is better to leave the fused patches in place. Consider purchasing a hooked rug with iron on patches only if they can be removed or are minimal in size and number and not aesthetically offensive. Price should reflect the poor attempt at repair.

Applying latex underneath or on top of iron on patches is lethal. Undoing that combination is nearly impossible. Avoid buying hand-hooked rugs in this condition.

The underside reveals that the aforementioned hooked rug was subjected to just about every bad quick fix repair imaginable including the use of duct tape, latex, and ironed on and glued on patches. Restoration is possible but will be costly and time consuming. Trying to undo or working around these failed attempts at repair are a restorer's nightmare.

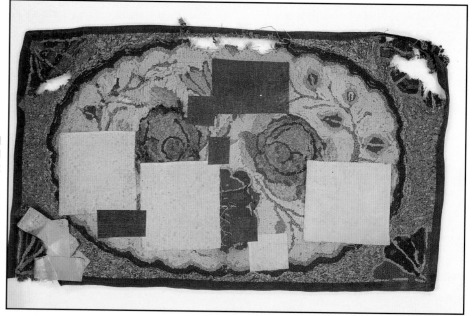

Hooked stripes of subdued and limited shades form a pleasing geometric pattern. The rug looks fine but when handled the edges are inflexible due to an application of glue around the perimeters; an easy but improper way to stop unraveling. Preprinted pattern. Of Canadian Maritime origins. 1920-1940. 22" x 37".

The underside corner of this geometric design hooked rug shows an ironed on binding that was later reattached with glue. The hasty and failed attempts at repair have left the edges of the rug stiff and hard to the touch.

PET STAINS

You may love Maxie and simply adore Muffie but you won't be pleased when the smell of pet urine starts wafting up from your prized hooked rug. A distinctive foul odor (cat urine is the worst), yellowish stains, and the random running of colors are indicators that an animal has left its mark.

Left untreated the unpleasant odor of urine lingers and beckons pets back to the scene of the crime. The acids in the urine will, over time, rot the rug's foundation and fabric loops.

When purchasing a hooked rug don't be afraid to use your nose. Sniff various areas of the rug and visually check for animal fur, stains, and colors that have bled. You may receive a few strange looks but rest assured what your nose barely notices at an outdoor flea market has the potential of reeking to high heaven inside your home on a hot and humid August afternoon. Avoid buying any hooked rugs that an animal has urinated on.

Should a pet accident occur immediately treat the area by blotting up any urine with a clean white cloth, paper towel or sponge. Remove any feces or vomit. Surface clean the area using a 50/50 solution of household white vinegar and water and a few drops of a mild liquid detergent or soap. Whisk the solution and use the foam and a small amount of the liquid to clean the affected area. Vinegar will neutralize the odor, stabilize the colors, and also discourage your pet from returning to the rug and wetting again.

In addition to urine stains, the random running of colors in limited areas is often an indicator that an animal has wet on a hooked rug. Cleaning will not remove the stains caused by the running colors and often does little for those from the urine. Preprinted pattern. 1950-1960. 15" x 26".

Chapter Ten

Cost: An Overall View

ANTIQUE HOOKED RUGS

The range of prices for antique hooked rugs is wide and varied. Design, age, size, condition, and desirability determine value and price. Most popular are primitive portrayals of animals. Those featuring people, houses, dates, patriotic themes, and whimsical sayings are also highly sought after and if in good condition can sell for thousands of dollars. Grenfell mats hooked in Newfoundland and Labrador during the early 1900s and in good condition start in the hundreds of dollars and reach into the thousands. Also popular and always in demand are choice geometric as well as floral designs. These also start in the hundreds and go up from there. The trade papers, the auction pages, a visit to shops and shows, and browsing on-line will give you a good idea of the variety and the range of prices that old hooked rugs are selling for. An educated collector can still find choice antique rugs at appealing prices, but with each passing year the search gets more difficult. Asking prices reflect the growing number of admirers and the limited supply.

Prices for antique hooked rugs of animals in good condition can reach into the thousands. An oval wreath of flowers, buds, and bunches of grapes frame a beloved dog. Ornate borders enhance the portrait. Possibly of Maine origins. 1870-1890. 29" x 53". A rug of this size, age, and theme, in good condition, could be expected to realize between $4,000 and $8,000 at a specialty auction or high-end show or shop. However, I would not be surprised to see such a rug sell for $20,000. *Courtesy of Sidney and Elizabeth Stewart.*

Hooked folk art is highly desirable and always sought after. Amid houses and lollipop trees, twin riders straddle oversized cats. Jute twine was vertically hooked to create the ochre background. 1900-1920. 18" x 35". A rug of this size, age, and theme, in good condition, could be expected to realize between $1,000 and $3,000 at a specialty auction or high-end show or shop.

Traditional floral designs are always popular and prices reflect aesthetic appeal, age, size, and condition. Prices for rugs of this genre start in the hundreds and go up. 1870-1890. 21" x 38". A rug of this size, age, and theme, in good condition, could be expected to realize between $400 and $800 at a specialty auction or high-end show or shop.

Some collectors prefer fanciful flowers that were hooked by imaginative rug makers. 1870-1890. 34" x 58". A rug of this size, age, and theme, in good condition, could be expected to realize between $400 and $800 at a specialty auction or high-end show or shop. *Collection of Sidney and Elizabeth Stewart.*

Prices for Grenfell mats in good condition, with strong color, and complete with an original Grenfell Labrador Industries label are valued in the hundreds and reach into the thousands. Early 20th century. 18.5" x 32". A rug of this size, age, and theme, in good condition, could be expected to realize between $1,000 and $2,000 at a specialty auction or high-end show or shop.

A hooked tribute to a special year. The reason for its significance is unknown. Dated 1908 and of the period. 37.5" x 64.75". A rug of this size, age, and theme, in good condition, could be expected to realize between $700 and $1,400 at a specialty auction or high-end show or shop.

COLLECTIBLE HOOKED RUGS

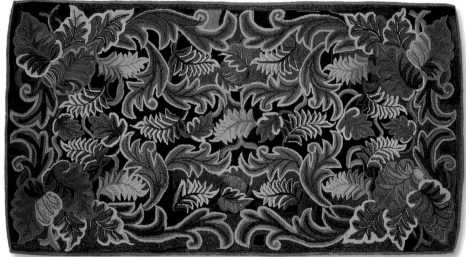

The best bargains to be had for hooked rugs can be found among those deemed collectible. With greater numbers available and of unlimited subject matter and often priced below their antique counterparts, collectible hooked rugs attract a continually expanding audience. You can spend less than $100 or well into the thousands. Prices are across-the-board. Design, age, size, and condition are all considered when determining value.

A jungle-like growth of leaves, ferns, and scrolls fills this vibrant rug. Hooked mainly of woolen yarns. 1910-1930. 37" x 70". A rug of this size, age, and theme, in good condition, could be expected to realize between $1,500 and $2,500 at a specialty auction or high-end show or shop. *Private Collection.*

Not yet ready to celebrate its 100th birthday, but desirable and delightful nonetheless. Rainbow and twin vases of flowers add tidings of gladness to a simple house framed in autumn leaves and braided edge. 1920-1940. 26" x 46". A rug of this size, age, and theme, in good condition, could be expected to realize between $1,500 and $2,500 at a specialty auction or high-end show or shop.

Perhaps hooked to signify the United States involvement in World War II, 1941 is surrounded by a more pleasant aspect of that historically important year. Could the flowers represent those found at the Pearl Harbor U. S. Naval base in Hawaii? An interesting rug of unusual color scheme. Price would reflect its damaged condition. Dated 1941 and of the period. 27" x 37". A rug of this size, age, and theme, in good condition, could be expected to realize between $100 and $400 at an auction, show, or shop. With damage such as this the price would drop to $50-$100.

A renewed interest in traditional floral and scroll design hooked rugs was evident by the large number of patterns printed in the 1930s, 40s, and 50s. At home in Victorian settings and sought out by interior decorators hooked rugs such as the one pictured are typically priced in the low hundreds and go up from there. 1930-1950. 33" x 57". A rug of this size, age, and theme, in good condition, could be expected to realize between $300 and $500 at a specialty auction or high-end show or shop.

CONTEMPORARY HOOKED RUGS

As contemporary hooking artists earn their place in the art world and their work is featured in galleries and museums, admiration grows and prices rise. Savvy collectors are acquiring modern hooked art for its aesthetic appeal as well as speculating on steadily increasing monetary values. Those deemed worthy of being called hooked art should be viewed, appraised, and priced as fine art.

Pictured are three hooked studies of French landmarks by noted Maryland artist Roslyn Logsdon. Selections from her portfolio start at $850.

"Montmajour," a 13th century medieval abbey on a hillside outside of Arles, France. Roslyn Logsdon. 2000. 29.5" x 20". *Courtesy of Roslyn Logsdon.*

A scene from Provence. Houses in "Rousillon" are tinted by the ochre that is mined in nearby hills. Roslyn Logsdon. 2001. 21" x 17". *Courtesy of Roslyn Logsdon.*

"Studio Through The Trees" captures the work place of French Impressionist, Paul Cézanne. Roslyn Logsdon. 2000. 33.5" x 24.5". *Courtesy of Roslyn Logsdon.*

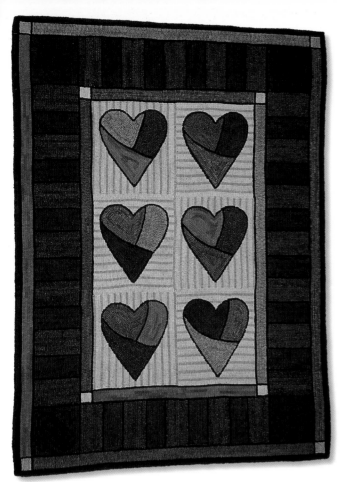

Contemporary rugs hooked for pleasure with no original intention of being perceived as fine art should be appreciated and valued as hand-made textiles. A time consuming project that requires patience, skill, and a bounty of materials, the making of a hooked rug is a true labor of love.

Using left over woolen fabrics from other projects, Canadian rug hooker Cathy Henning enjoyed hooking this divided heart design. She adapted the pattern from a note card of an unknown artist. Like many rug makers, Cathy hooks to please herself, her family, and friends, selling an occasional rug along the way. 2002. 42" x 32". *Courtesy of Cathy Henning.*

"Hound Dog Pillow" sits on a couch in the den. Dick LaBarge pattern hooked by Cathy Henning. 2001. 8" x 12". *Courtesy of Cathy Henning.*

Everyone has a "Bad Day At The Office." Designed and hooked by Cathy Henning. 2000. 18" x 15". *Courtesy of Cathy Henning.*

Commissioned work is generally charged on a per square foot fee. Prices start at $100 a square foot and go up. The finer the strip of material hooked and the more complex the design, the longer it takes to complete the job. Per square foot fees generally cover design consultation, labor, and all materials.

Some rug hooking artists will accept commissioned work but do not charge by the foot. The prices they ask reflect their artistic talent as well as the popularity of their work. Some believe, and rightfully so, that creativity cannot be measured by a yardstick.

"Starry Night In Greenport" pictures New York's Long Island community after dark and was commissioned by a van Gogh lover. Woolen fabrics and silk and woolen yarns on monk's cloth. Gail F. Horton. 1997. 25" x 33". From the Collection of David Berson. *Courtesy of Gail F. Horton.*

"Bruce's Café With Scorpio" was commissioned by restaurant owner Bruce Bollman and used to advertise a favorite Greenport eatery. Gail F. Horton. 22" x 57". *Courtesy of Gail F. Horton.*

Chapter Eleven

Care

Hand-hooked rugs require and deserve special care. Treated properly they will reward you with long life and increased monetary value.

Light cleaning can be accomplished by gently sweeping the front and back sides of your rug with a broom or soft bristle brush. A hand pushed carpet sweeper also works well. Turn your rugs upside down and walk on them this way for a few days. Trapped dirt will fall to the floor and then can easily be swept up. Do not use a vacuum cleaner. Vacuuming can severely damage your rug. Refrain from shaking or beating. Sharp jerking motions can break the threads of the rug's woven foundation. This is particularly true for older hooked rugs.

Low cost to buy, no cost to run, and a hooked rug's best friend; the lowly carpet sweeper unsung and resting in the doorway after a job well done. The use of a broom or carpet sweeper will greatly prolong the life of any hooked rug. And don't forget the health benefits of sweeping aerobics. A preprinted pattern. 1920-1940. Dimensions unavailable.

Visible along this rug's edges are the early signs of vacuum cleaner damage. The amount of damage increases as the vacuuming continues. Preprinted pattern. Of Canadian Maritime origins. 1940-1950. 23" x 40".

Take a lesson from your grandmother and air your hooked rugs outside on the grass for a few hours. Sunshine and fresh breezes combined with the natural deodorizing power of green grass will leave your rugs smelling fresh and clean. A short time in direct sunlight should not cause fabrics to fade. Two months of strong exposure will. Hand-hooked rugs do not benefit from being left out in the rain. Prolonged exposure to moisture will rot foundation fibers.

Another old-fashioned tried and true method of cleaning is to take advantage of Mother Nature. Sprinkle a thin layer of light and fluffy snow over the top of your hooked rug. Let it remain in place for a few minutes then gently broom sweep clean keeping the rug flat. Repeat the process on the rug's other side.

To keep your hooked rugs in the best possible condition they should not be subjected to pet traffic. A dog's nails and a cat's claws can cause damage. If you choose to share your hooked rugs with family pets and broom or carpet sweeping fails to remove all the fur, wiping the rug with a damp sponge will remove the residue of unwanted hair. Regularly air any hooked rugs that are in contact with animals.

Give your rugs a thorough cleaning once a year using a mild soap and water solution or shampoo made expressly for hooked rugs. Begin by gently sweeping both sides of the rug to remove any loose dirt. Mix up a solution of cold water and just enough soap (mild liquid detergent works well) to form suds. A small amount of white vinegar can also be added. Vinegar is a natural cleaner, and deodorant, and acts as a mordant for colors that tend to bleed. Before cleaning you must test for colorfastness. Lay your rug flat with the wrong side up. Using a piece of white cotton cloth and the suds and small amount of liquid daub the rug's various colors. If the colors bleed it's best to discover the problem on the underside of the rug. Allow the test areas to dry for at least 24 hours. If all fabrics are colorfast, proceed with cleaning the front surface. With a soft brush or white cotton cloth, gently scrub in small circular motions, using the suds and as little of the water as possible. When the process is completed, blot up any excess moisture with a white towel. Lay the rug flat until completely dry. Do not hang a damp hooked rug on a rod or clothesline. Repeat the process on the underside of the rug. If needed, repeat the cleaning procedure on heavily stained areas.

Never wash any hand-hooked rug in a washing machine. The results will be disastrous and most always the rug is ruined beyond repair. Do not submerge your rug in the bathtub or hose it down on the driveway. The threads of the burlap base are likely to rot from the soaking.

While outside for an airing visually and physically inspect your hooked rugs for signs of wear and tear. Small holes are easier and less expensive to fix than big holes. 1870-1880. 74" x 76". *Courtesy of Sidney and Elizabeth Stewart.*

Newer linen and cotton foundations are stronger but also should not be soaked in water.

Hand-hooked rugs cannot withstand the rigorous scrubbing and harsh chemicals used to clean commercial grade carpeting. All hand-hooked rugs should be cleaned by hand. If you are sending your rugs out to be cleaned make sure the person is qualified. Ask questions. If you know more than the "professionals" do when it comes to hand-hooked rugs it would be wise to go elsewhere or clean the rugs yourself.

During your search for rugs ask for the name of a hooked rug restorer. Antique dealers will know who does the best repairs and cleaning.

DISPLAY

If hooked rugs are used on wooden floors it is wise to place a good quality pad underneath to prevent slipping. Carpet stores carry a wide variety of pads that can be custom cut to fit any size rug.

Hooked rugs add a touch of color, softness, and warmth to wooden floors. A good quality underpad will prevent slipping. 1900-1920. 32" x 51".

If you wish to display your hooked rug on the wall simply hand sew a fabric sleeve on the back. Insert a rod or wooden dowel and hang as you would a curtain or other textile wall hanging.

You may choose to mount your hooked rug and hang it as you would a painting. Preferred by many collectors, rugs are mounted for both visual effect and preservation purposes. First select a sturdy fabric that will serve as a backing. The color should highlight or blend with the colors of your rug. Allow for enough fabric so that when placed in the middle of the backing there is at least eight inches of fabric extending beyond all four perimeters of the rug. With the rug right side up and placed in the middle of the backing, hand sew the rug to the backing using a strong color coordinated thread. Make sure your stitches firmly secure the rug to the fabric backing yet are small enough to go undetected. Hide the stitches in between the hooked loops. Sew around the entire rug as well as reinforcing center areas to prevent sagging when the rug is hung. Once the sewing is completed the backing is pulled taut and secured to wooden stretcher bars (available at art supply stores) using a heavy-duty staple gun. Trim any excess fabric. Mounting a hooked rug does require time, skill, and patience but the results are well worth the effort. Most professional framers will be able to properly mount your hooked rug. Make sure the framer does not use glue or latex to secure the rug to the fabric backing or the stretcher bars.

Mounted and ready to hang. The fabric chosen to mount this mirror image composition of deer, birds, and flowers complements the colors within and does not draw attention away from the hooked work. Of New England origins. 1870-1890. 20.5" x 48.5". *Private Collection*.

Hooked rugs are mounted for both visual effect and preservation purposes. Twisting vine with leaves and flowers. Of New England origins. 1890-1910. 29" x 51". *Private Collection*.

A Grenfell mat, unusual in its geometric design, was mounted on fabric of contrasting color. Doing so visually makes the soft tones of the mat appear brighter. Grenfell Labrador Industries. Early 20th century. 31.5" x 16".

Undetectable hand stitching secures the Grenfell mat to the fabric on which it is mounted.

Small hooked rugs and mats bring a welcomed touch of color to a wide variety of surfaces such as tables and bureaus. They can easily be moved around to suit your decorating needs.

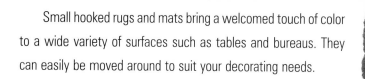

A gift from a friend recalls happy days spent in the Cape Breton region of Nova Scotia. Chéticamp made. 1990s. 4" x 4".

Tourist traveling through Cape Breton often returned home with small Chéticamp mats tucked in their suitcases. Round mats were placed under lamps and vases and were also used to decorate chairs. 1930-1950. Diameter 10".

The Grenfell Labrador Industries made many small tabletop mats that were sold in the United States, England, and Canada. Early 20th century. Diameter 8".

For those who love hooked rugs and wish to be constantly in their presence, hooking artist Susan Smidt has created wearable hooked art. Her palm-size pins, priced between $20 and $40, celebrate life with realistic, whimsical, and abstract themes. Handmade from start to finish, production is limited. When available the smile provoking hooked miniatures sell out quickly and are treasured by those who wear them.

Hooking artist Susan Smidt enjoys an occasional break from hooking her large abstracts and creates miniatures; each small enough to fit in your pocket. 1998-2001. *Courtesy of Susan Smidt.*

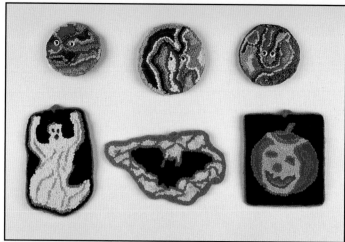

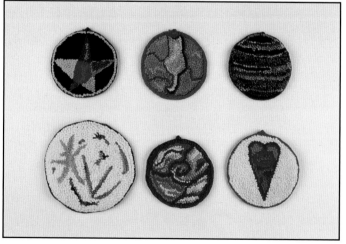

Wearable art. Hooked pins by Susan Smidt.
1998-2003. *Courtesy of Susan Smidt.*

As your collection grows you might want to consider having your rugs appraised as well as insured. Contact an appraiser who is familiar with hooked rugs and offers an affidavit of his or her credentials. Insurance companies will not accept your opinion or that of your next door neighbor. Take photographs of all your hooked rugs. Record the size, age, date purchased, and price paid. If the rug is one you designed and hooked include your name, where the rug was made, materials used (such as wool on linen), and date the rug was completed. If the rug took several years to finish or was made to honor a special occasion make note of that information. If not of original design also include the name of the pattern and identify the pattern maker. It's best to keep the photos, information, and copies of any appraisals together in a safe place such as a fireproof container or bank safety deposit box.

With each passing year antique hooked rugs increase in monetary value. Polychrome concentric rectangles frame a center scroll and peacock tail motif.1880-1900. 35" x 52". A rug of this size, age, and theme, in good condition, could be expected to realize between $800 and $1,200 at a specialty auction or high-end show or shop. *Private Collection*.

Grenfell mats are among the most expensive hooked rugs sold today with prices soaring into the thousands. Should your collection include exceptional Grenfell mats such as this scene of a polar bear on an ice flow you should have the pieces appraised and insured. Early 20th century. 26.5" x 40". A rug of this size, age, and theme, in good condition, could be expected to realize between $2,000 and $5,000 at a specialty auction or high-end show or shop. *Private Collection*

Fine art, whether painted or hooked, should be valued as works of art. "Lounging." Roslyn Logsdon. 2000. 18" x 27". *Courtesy of Roslyn Logsdon.*

Insuring for replacement value covers the cost to have your rugs reproduced should they be stolen or destroyed. Hours of intensive labor and yards of woolen fabric of many colors are required to hook flowers such as these. Center detail of 9' x12' hooked rug that took eight years to complete. 1950-1960.

Designed and hooked by Canadian rug maker Margaret Hunt Wilson "Caswell Border Rug" was inspired by the embroidered Caswell Carpet from the Metropolitan Museum of Art in New York City. Both interesting in design and beautiful in its craftsmanship, the large rug was four years in the making. In case of loss finding a similar rug would be impossible. Replicating a rug of this size and quality would be very difficult and expensive. Such a rug should be insured for replacement value with cost for labor and materials upgraded every few years. 1978-1982. 6.5' x 8.5'. *Courtesy of Margaret Hunt Wilson.*

And so now you know my secrets. Toss your concerns to the wind. Go out and find some hooked rugs to collect. Good luck and happy hunting! From the Ralph Burnham Collection. 1890-1910. 19" x 35".

Endnotes

Chapter 5. Where To Find Antique and Collectible Hooked Rugs

1. Emma Tennant, *Rag Rugs of England and America* (London: Walker Books,1992), 82.

2. Jean Leymarie, *The Jerusalem Windows* (New York: George Brazzler, 1967).

3. Ibid.

4. Magdelana Dabrowsky, *Kandinsky Compositions – Exhibition Catalog.* (New York: Museum of Modern Art, 1995).

Chapter 9. Pests and Problems- What to Buy – What to Avoid

1.Hilary Dole Klein and Adrian M. Wenner, *Tiny Game Hunting – Environmentally Healthy Ways to Trap and Kill Pests in Your House and Garden* (Berkley: University of California Press, 2001) 28.

Suggested Reading

Beatty, Alice, and Mary Sargent. *Basic Rug Hooking*. Harrisburg, Pennsylvania: Stackpole Books, 1990.

Brown, Barbara Evans. *Preserving the Past in Primitive Rugs. Rug Hooking Magazine's Framework Series*. Harrisburg, Pennsylvania. 1999.

Burton, Mary Sheppard. *A Passion for the Creative Life: Textiles to Lift the Spirit.* Germantown, Maryland: Sign of the Hook Books, 2002.

Crouse, Gloria. *Hooking Rugs: New materials, New techniques* (and companion video). Newtown, Connecticut: The Tauton Press, 1990.

Field, Jeanne. *Shading Flowers: The Complete Guide for Rug Hookers*. Harrisburg, Pennsylvania: Stackpole Books, 1991.

Fitzpatrick, Deanne. *Hook Me A Story: The History and Method of Rug Hooking in Atlantic Canada.* Halifax, Nova Scotia: Nimbus Publishing, 1999.

Kent, William.W. *The Hooked Rug*. New York: Tudor Publishing Company, 1930.

_____. *Hooked Rug Design*. Springfield, Massachusetts: The Pond-Ekberg Company, 1949.

_____. *Rare Hooked Rugs*. Springfield, Massachusetts: The Pond Ekberg Company, 1941.

Kopp, Joel and Kate. *American Hooked and Sewn Rugs: Folk Art Underfoot*. New York: E. P. Dutton, Inc., 1985.

Lais, Emma Lou, and Barbara Carroll. *Antique Colours for Primitive Rugs: Formulas Using Cushing Acid Dyes*. Kennebunkport, Maine: W. Cushing & Company, 1996.

_____. *American Primitive Hooked Rugs: Primer for Recreating Antique Rugs*. Kennebunkport, Maine: Wildwood Press, 1999.

Lincoln, Maryanne. *Recipes From the Dye Kitchen. Rug Hooking Magazine's Framework Series*. Harrisburg, Pennsylvania: 1999.

Linsley, Leslie. *Hooked Rugs: An American Folk Art*. New York, New York: Clarkson N. Potter, 1992.

Logsdon, Roslyn. *People and Places: Roslyn Logsdon's Imagery in Fiber. Rug Hooking Magazine's Framework Series.* Harrisburg, Pennsylvania, 1998.

McGown, Pearl K. *Color in Hooked Rugs*. Boston: Buck Printing Co., 1954. 1954.

_____. *Dreams Beneath the Designs*. Boston: Bruce Humphries Inc., 1939.

_____. *The Lore and Lure of Hooked Rugs.* Acton, Massachusetts: Acton Press, 1966.

_____. *You…Can Hook Rugs.* Boston: Buck Printing Co., 1951.

Moshimer, Joan. *The Complete Rug Hooker*. Boston: New York Graphic Society, 1975.

_____. *Hooked On Cats: Complete patterns and instructions for rug hookers*. Harrisburg, Pennsylvania: Stackpole Books, 1991.

Oxford, Amy. *Punch Needle Rug Hooking: Techniques and Designs*. Atglen, Pennsylvania: Schiffer Publishing Ltd., 2003.

Rex, Stella H. *Practical Hooked Rugs*. Ashville, Maine: Cobblesmith, 1975.

Stratton, Charlotte K. *Rug Hooking Made Easy*. New York: Harper and Brothers Publishing, 1955.

Tennant, Emma. *Rag Rugs of England and America.* London: Walker Books, 1992.

Turbayne, Jessie A. *Hooked Rugs: History and the Continuing Tradition*. West Chester, Pennsylvania: Schiffer Publishing Ltd., 1991.

_____. *Hooked Rug Treasury*. Atglen, Pennsylvania: Schiffer Publishing Ltd. 1997.

_____. *The Hooker's Art.* Atglen, Pennsylvania: Schiffer Publishing, 1993.

Waugh, Elizabeth. *Collecting Hooked Rugs*. New York: The Century Company, 1927.